Additional Practice
Workbook
GRADE 8

enVision® Mathematics

SAVVAS
LEARNING COMPANY

ISBN-13: 978-1-4182-6922-7
ISBN-10: 1-4182-6922-0

6 21

rade 8
pics 1–8

pic 1 Real Numbers

pic 2 Analyze and Solve Linear Equations

pic 3 Use Functions to Model Relationships

pic 4 Investigate Bivariate Data

Topic 5 **Analyze and Solve Systems of Linear Equations**

Topic 6 **Congruence and Similarity**

Topic 7 **Understand and Apply the Pythagorean Theorem**

Topic 8 **Solve Problems Involving Surface Area and Volume**

1-1 Additional Practice

Scan for
Multimedia

Leveled Practice In **1–4**, write the decimal as a fraction or mixed number.

1. Write $0.\overline{2}$ as a fraction.

Let $x =$ ☐.

$10x =$ ☐

$10x - x =$ ☐ $-$ ☐

$9x =$ ☐

$x =$ ☐

So $0.\overline{2}$ is equal to ☐.

2. Write $1.888...$ as a mixed number.

Let $x =$ ☐.

$10x =$ ☐

$10x - x =$ ☐ $-$ ☐

$9x =$ ☐

$x =$ ☐

So $1.888...$ is equal to ☐.

3. Write $0.4\overline{6}$ as a fraction.

Let $x =$ ☐.

$10x =$ ☐

$100x =$ ☐

$100x - 10x =$ ☐ $-$ ☐

$90x =$ ☐

$x =$ ☐

So $0.4\overline{6}$ is equal to ☐.

4. Write $0.\overline{12}$ as a fraction.

Let $x =$ ☐.

$100x =$ ☐

$100x - x =$ ☐ $-$ ☐

$99x =$ ☐

$x =$ ☐

So $0.\overline{12}$ is equal to ☐.

5. Look for Relationships Brianna asked 45 students if they would vote for her to be student council president. She used her calculator to compare the number of students who said yes with the total number of students. Her calculator showed the result as $0.6222...$.

a. Write this number as a fraction.

b. How many students said they would vote for Brianna?

6. Write $3.0\overline{1}$ as a mixed number.

7. Write $0.\overline{7}$ as a fraction.

8. Higher Order Thinking A reporter determines a baseball player's batting average, which is a ratio of number of hits to number of times at bats. The result is shown on a calculator as 0.2121....

   a. Write this repeating decimal as a fraction.

   b. How many hits would the player be expected to get in 200 at bats? Explain.

9. Write $0.\overline{32}$ as a fraction.

10. Write $2.\overline{5}$ as a mixed number.

✅ Assessment Practice

11. Choose the repeating decimal that is equal to the fraction on the left.

	$0.2\overline{4}$	$0.3\overline{6}$	$0.\overline{24}$	$0.\overline{36}$
$\frac{33}{90}$	☐	☐	☐	☐
$\frac{24}{99}$	☐	☐	☐	☐
$\frac{36}{99}$	☐	☐	☐	☐
$\frac{22}{90}$	☐	☐	☐	☐

12. What fraction is equivalent to $0.\overline{6}$?

Name: _____

1-2 Additional Practice

1. Is 8.141141114... a rational or irrational number? Explain.

2. Is $\sqrt{72}$ rational or irrational? Explain.

3. Which numbers are rational?

$\sqrt{81}, \sqrt{50}, -12, 0, \frac{12}{5}, 6.\overline{54}$

4. Which numbers are irrational?

$11, \sqrt{15}, -14, \frac{5}{7}, \frac{9}{4}, 0.151155111555...$

5. Richie says that 2.141441444... is a rational number. Elsa disagrees.

a. Who is correct?

b. What is the likely cause of the error?

6. **Reasoning** Write the side length of the square as a square root. Is the side length a rational number? Explain.

$$A = 121 \text{ ft}^2$$

7. Keisha writes the following list of numbers.

   -9, $\sqrt{8}$, 3.0, $\frac{2}{5}$, $2.4\overline{2}$, π

   a. Which numbers are rational?

   b. Which numbers are irrational?

8. **Higher Order Thinking** You are given the expressions $\sqrt{60 + n}$ and $\sqrt{2n + 28}$. What is tthe smallest value of n that will make each number rational?

✓ Assessment Practice

9. Which numbers are rational?

   I. $3.222222...$

   II. $0.112123123412345...$

   III. 1.589

   Ⓐ I only

   Ⓑ II only

   Ⓒ III only

   Ⓓ I and III

   Ⓔ II and III

   Ⓕ None of the above

10. Classify the following numbers as rational or irrational.

    $\frac{2}{3}$ $3.1415926535...$ 0 $\sqrt{1}$ $7.\overline{4}$ 15 $\sqrt{3}$

Rational	Irrational

1-3 Additional Practice

PRACTICE   TUTORIAL

Scan for Multimedia

Leveled Practice In **1** and **2**, find the rational approximation.

1. Approximate using perfect squares.

$\boxed{} < 78 < \boxed{}$

$\boxed{} < \sqrt{78} < \boxed{}$

$\boxed{} < \sqrt{78} < \boxed{}$

So $\sqrt{78}$ is between $\boxed{}$ and $\boxed{}$.

2. Find the rational approximation of $\sqrt{37}$.

a. Approximate using perfect squares.

$\boxed{} < 37 < \boxed{}$

$\boxed{} < \sqrt{37} < \boxed{}$

$\boxed{} < \sqrt{37} < \boxed{}$

b. **Model with Math** Locate and plot $\sqrt{37}$ on a number line. Find a better approximation using decimals.

$6.0 \times 6.0 = \boxed{}$

$6.1 \times 6.1 = \boxed{}$

$\sqrt{37}$ is closer to $\boxed{}$.

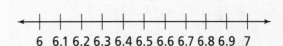

6   6.1 6.2 6.3 6.4 6.5 6.6 6.7 6.8 6.9 7

3. **Reasoning** Compare $-\sqrt{7}$ and $-3.12345...$. Justify your reasoning.

4. Does $\frac{22}{7}$, -3, $\sqrt{17}$, $\frac{16}{5}$, or -4.5 come first when the numbers are listed from least to greatest? Explain.

5. List the numbers in order from least to greatest.

$\sqrt{5}$, 3.7, $\frac{1}{2}$, -4, $-\frac{9}{4}$

6. Compare 6.51326... and $\sqrt{39}$. Show your work.

7. Ross is comparing $\sqrt{11}$ and $5.\overline{4}$. He says that $\sqrt{11} > 5.\overline{4}$ because $\sqrt{11} = 5.5$.

   a. What is the correct comparison?

   b. **Critique Reasoning** What mistake did Ross likely make?

8. **Higher Order Thinking** If $x = 5$, $y = 6$, and $z = 2$, is $\sqrt{x^2 + y^2 + z^2 + 50}$ rational or irrational? Explain.

✓ Assessment Practice

9. Which list shows the numbers in order from least to greatest?

   Ⓐ $\sqrt{32}$, 5.2, $4\frac{2}{3}$, $\sqrt{17}$

   Ⓑ $\sqrt{17}$, $4\frac{2}{3}$, 5.2, $\sqrt{32}$

   Ⓒ $4\frac{2}{3}$, $\sqrt{32}$, $\sqrt{17}$, 5.2

   Ⓓ 5.2, $\sqrt{17}$, $\sqrt{32}$, $4\frac{2}{3}$

10. The area of a square picture frame is 55 square inches. Find the length of one side of the frame. Explain.

    PART A

    To the nearest whole inch

    PART B

    To the nearest tenth of an inch

1-4 Additional Practice

Leveled Practice In **1** and **2**, evaluate the square root or cube root.

1. Relate the area of the square to the length of each side.

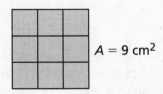

$A = 9$ cm^2

Side length   Side length

⬚ cm   ×   ⬚ cm

$\sqrt{9} = $ ⬚

2. Relate the volume of the cube to the length of each edge.

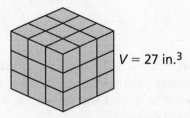

$V = 27$ in.^{3}

Edge length   Edge length   Edge length

⬚ in.   ×   ⬚ in.   ×   ⬚ in.

$\sqrt[3]{27} = $ ⬚

3. Ms. Lu is adding a new room to her house. The room will be a cube with volume 4,913 cubic feet. What is the length of the new room?

4. The volume of a box for earrings is 216 cubic centimeters. What is the length of one edge of the box?

5. The area of a square garage is 121 square feet. Will it fit a car that measures 13 feet long? Explain.

6. Nadia wants to enclose a square garden with fencing. It has an area of 141 square feet. To the nearest foot, how much fencing will she need? Explain.

7. Benjamin rents a storage unit that is shaped like a cube. There are 12 identical storage units in each row of the facility. If each storage unit has a volume of 125 cubic feet, what is the length of each row in the facility?

8. Would you classify the number 55 as a perfect square, as a perfect cube, both, or neither? Explain.

9. **Critique Reasoning** Clara says that if you square the number 4 and then divide the result by 2, you end up with 4. Is Clara correct? Explain.

10. **Higher Order Thinking** A fish tank at an aquarium has a volume of 1,568 cubic feet and a depth of 8 feet. If the base of the tank is square, what is the length of each side of the tank?

Assessment Practice

11. Which expression has the least value?

    Ⓐ $\sqrt{81} \cdot 2$

    Ⓑ $\sqrt{81} - \sqrt{25}$

    Ⓒ $\sqrt{64} + \sqrt{25}$

    Ⓓ $\sqrt{64} - 3$

12. On a math test, Ana writes 9 as the solution to $\sqrt[3]{27}$.

    PART A

    Find the correct solution.

    PART B

    What error did Ana likely make on the test?

    Ⓐ Ana cubed 27.

    Ⓑ Ana divided 27 by 3.

    Ⓒ Ana multiplied 27 by 3.

    Ⓓ Ana cubed 3.

Name: _____

1-5 Additional Practice

Scan for
Multimedia

PRACTICE   TUTORIAL

Leveled Practice In **1** and **2**, solve.

1. $y^2 = 169$

$$\sqrt{\boxed{}} = \pm\sqrt{\boxed{}}$$

$$z = \pm \boxed{}$$

The solutions are $\boxed{}$ and $\boxed{}$.

2. $b^3 = 1{,}000$

$$\sqrt[3]{\boxed{}} = \sqrt[3]{\boxed{}}$$

$$b = \boxed{}$$

3. The volume of a cube shaped crate is 27 cubic feet. What is the length of one edge of the crate?

4. The area of a square patio is 196 square feet. How long is each side of the patio?

5. Solve the equation $c^2 = 4$.

6. Solve the equation $x^2 = 80$.

7. Solve the equation $r^3 = 216$.

8. Solve the equation $v^3 = 36$.

9. Jasmine is a structural engineer. She designs the lift hill of a roller coaster that models the equation $y = x^3$, where y is the height and x is the length from the start of the lift hill. Using this model, how far from the start of the lift hill does the ride reach a height of 343 meters?

10. **Higher Order Thinking** Holly wants to make a frame for a painting. The painting is square and has an area of 225 square inches.

    a. Write an equation to represent the area of the painting, using s for side length. Then, solve the equation for s.

    b. The framing material costs $1.35 per inch. How much will she spend?

☑ Assessment Practice

11. On a recent homework assignment, Eli needed to solve the equation $g^2 = 49$. He incorrectly wrote $g = -7$.

    PART A

    What is the correct solution?

    PART B

    Critique Reasoning What error did Eli likely make?

    Ⓐ He did not take the square root of 49 correctly since $(-7)^2 \neq 49$.

    Ⓑ He did not solve the equation completely since there is a positive solution as well.

    Ⓒ He did not solve the equation completely since there are two positive solutions.

    Ⓓ He did not solve the equation completely since there are two negative solutions.

12. The zoo is building a new tank for some of its fish. The tank will be a cube able to hold 3,375 cubic feet of water.

    PART A

    Which equation could you use to find the length of each side of the tank?

    Ⓐ $3V = 3,375$

    Ⓑ $\frac{3,375}{3} = s$

    Ⓒ $V^3 = 3,375$

    Ⓓ $3,375 = s^3$

    PART B

    How long is each side of the tank?

Name: _____

1-6 Additional Practice

Leveled Practice In 1–4, use the properties of exponents to write an equivalent expression for each given expression.

1. $5^3 \cdot 5^4 = 5^{3\,\boxed{}\,4}$

$= \boxed{}^{\boxed{}}$

2. $\dfrac{4^9}{4^3} = 4^{9\,\boxed{}\,3}$

$= \boxed{}^{\boxed{}}$

3. $(7^2)^6 = 7^{2\,\boxed{}\,6}$

$= \boxed{}^{\boxed{}}$

4. $2^4 \cdot 6^4 = (\boxed{} \cdot \boxed{})^4$

$= \boxed{}^{\boxed{}}$

5. Simplify the expression $(x^{12})^3$.

6. Simplify the expression $(-12c^5)(3c^4)$.

7. Use the properties of exponents to simplify the expression $\dfrac{5^{22}}{5^{13}}$.

8. Use the properties of exponents to write an equivalent expression for $(3 \cdot 6)^2$.

9. Make Sense and Persevere Compare the two expressions.

   a. Is the expression $a^{12} \cdot a^4$ equivalent to $a^8 \cdot a^8$? Explain.

   b. Does $a^{12} \cdot a^4 = a^8 \cdot a^8$ for all values of a? Explain.

10. A company manufactures photo cells. It uses the expression $(2x^3)^3$ millimeters per second to calculate the maximum capacity of a photo cell with area x^3 square millimeters. Use a property of exponents to simplify this expression.

11. a. Use a property of exponents to write $(2m)^4$ as a product of powers.

    b. **Generalize** Describe the property of exponents that you used.

12. **Higher Order Thinking** Find the two integers, m and n, that make the equation $(2x^n y^2)^m = 4x^6 y^4$ true.

☑ Assessment Practice

13. Select all the expressions equivalent to $(4x^5)(5x^6)$.

    ☐ $(2x^5)(10x^6)$

    ☐ $(4x^5)(6x^5)$

    ☐ $(4x^6)(5x^5)$

    ☐ $20x^{11}$

    ☐ $20x^{30}$

14. You are given the expression $\frac{12^8}{12^4}$ to simplify.

    PART A

    Which equation shows the correct property of exponents to use?

    Ⓐ $\frac{a^m}{a^n} = a^{m+n}$

    Ⓑ $\frac{a^m}{a^n} = a^{m-n}$

    Ⓒ $\frac{a^m}{a^n} = a^{m-a}$

    Ⓓ $\frac{a^m}{a^n} = a^{n-m}$

    PART B

    Simplify the expression. Write your answer using exponential notation.

Name: _____

1-7 Additional Practice

1. Leveled Practice Complete the table to simplify the expression.

Given	Positive Exponent Form	Expanded Form				Simplified Form
5^{-4}	$\dfrac{1}{\boxed{}^{\boxed{}}}$	$\dfrac{1}{\boxed{} \times \boxed{} \times \boxed{} \times \boxed{}}$				$\dfrac{1}{\boxed{}}$

In 2–5, simplify each expression.

2. $135(z^0)$

3. $\dfrac{8}{9^0}$

4. $7^{-2}(-3)^2$

5. $\dfrac{a^{-3}}{b^{-2}}$, for $a = 5$ and $b = 6$.

In 6 and 7, compare the values using >, <, or =.

6. $\left(\dfrac{12}{65}\right)^0 \boxed{}$ 1

7. $52^{-4} \boxed{}$ 1

In 8 and 9, simplify each expression.

8. $9x^2y^{-3}$, for $x = 5$ and $y = 3$.

9. $14x^{-2}$, for $x = 7$.

10. Julia has to evaluate the expression 4^{-3} before she can join her classmates outside. She decides to use the value of the expression to help choose which activity to do. If the value is greater than 1, she will play basketball. If the value is equal to 1, she will play soccer. If the value is less than 1, she will play tennis. Which activity is Julia going to do today? Explain.

11. You are given the expression -6^{-4}.

   a. Rewrite the expression using a positive exponent.

   b. Reasoning Simplify the expression -6^{-4}. Is the result the same as simplifying the expression $(-6)^{-4}$? Explain.

12. Higher Order Thinking

   a. Is the value of the expression $\left(\frac{1}{4^{-2}}\right)^3$ greater than 1, equal to 1 or less than 1?

   b. If the value of the expression is greater than 1, show how you can change one sign to make the value less than 1. If the value is less than 1, show how you can change one sign to make the value greater than 1. If the value is equal to 1, show how you can make one change to make the value not equal to 1.

13. Construct Arguments Simplify the expression $18p^0$, assuming that p is nonzero. Will the value of the expression change with different values for p?

✅ Assessment Practice

14. Which expressions are equal to 10^{-5}? Select all that apply.

   ☐ 10^5

   ☐ $10{,}000$

   ☐ $10{,}000^{-5}$

   ☐ $\frac{1}{10^5}$

   ☐ $\frac{1}{10{,}000}$

15. Which expressions have a value less than 1 when $x = 3$? Select all that apply.

   ☐ $\left(\frac{3}{x^2}\right)^0$

   ☐ $\frac{x^0}{3^2}$

   ☐ $\frac{1}{6^{-x}}$

   ☐ $\frac{1}{x^{-3}}$

   ☐ $3x^{-4}$

Name: _____

1-8 Additional Practice

Scan for Multimedia

Leveled Practice In **1–3**, use powers of 10 to estimate quantities.

1. Use a single digit times a power of 10 to estimate the number 0.000007328.

   Rounded to the nearest millionth, the number is about ⬚.

   Written as the product of a single digit and a power of ten, this number is ⬚ × 10^⬚.

2. A city has a population of 38,802,500 people. Estimate this population to the nearest ten million.

   Rounded to the nearest ten million, the population is about ⬚.

   Written as the product of a single digit and a power of ten, this number is ⬚ × 10^⬚.

3. The mass of Planet X is 8.46×10^{22} kilograms. The mass of Planet Y is 5,028,000,000,000,000,000,000 kilograms. How many times greater is the mass of Planet X than the mass of Planet Y?

   The mass of Planet Y is about ⬚ × ⬚^⬚ kilograms.

   The mass of Planet X is about ⬚ × ⬚^⬚ kilograms.

   The mass of Planet X is about ⬚ times greater than that of Planet Y.

4. According to a survey, the residents of Country A have approximately 179,300,000 dogs and cats as pets. The same survey reports there are about 5.01×10^7 dogs and cats as pets in Country B. About how many times greater is the number of dogs and cats in Country A than Country B?

5. Estimate 0.00792398 to the nearest thousandth. Express your answer as a single digit times a power of ten.

6. Which number has the greater value, 7×10^{-9} or 6×10^{-4}?

7. On a certain planet, Continent X has an area of 6.23×10^6 square miles and Continent Y has an area of 63,600,000 square miles. How many time larger is Continent Y than Continent X?

8. Dion made $67,785 last year. Express this number as a single digit times a power of ten rounded to the nearest ten thousand.

9. A rectangle has length 8×10^4 millimeters and width 4×10^4 millimeters. How many times greater is the rectangle's length than width?

10. **Construct Arguments** Tara incorrectly estimates 36,591,000,000 meters as 4×10^6 meters. Is she correct? Explain.

11. **Higher Order Thinking** An astronomical unit (AU) is equal to the average distance from the Sun to Earth.

    a. An astronomical unit is about 92,955,807 miles. Use a single digit times a power of ten to estimate this value to the nearest ten million miles.

    b. Venus is about 7.2×10^{-1} AU from the Sun. Mars is about 1.5 AU from the Sun. Which planet is closest to Earth?

☑ Assessment Practice

12. The oldest rocks on Earth are about 4×10^9 years old. For which of these ages could this be an approximation?

    Ⓐ 0.000000004 years

    Ⓑ 3.45×10^9 years

    Ⓒ 3.349999999×10^9 years

    Ⓓ 4,149,000,000 years

13. Express 0.000000648 as a single digit times a power of ten rounded to the nearest ten millionth.

Name: _____

1-9 Additional Practice

Leveled Practice In **1** and **2**, complete the sentences.

1. Express the number 7.901×10^{12} in standard form.

   a. To change this number to standard form, move the decimal

   point ☐ places to the ☐.

   b. 7.901×10^{12} is written as ☐ in standard form.

2. You want to express 437,000 in scientific notation. What is the first step?

   a. To change this number to scientific notation, move the

   decimal point ☐ places to the ☐.

   b. 437,000 is written as ☐ × 10☐ in scientific notation.

3. Is 23×10^{-6} written in scientific notation? Justify your response.

4. Is 1.75×10^{6} written in scientific notation? Justify your response.

5. Your calculator display shows 5.3E − 9. Express the number in standard form.

6. Express the number 621,000 in scientific notation.

7. Express the number 0.00000001073 in scientific notation.

8. Express the number 5.2×10^{6} in standard form.

9. Express the number 8.5×10^5 in standard form.

10. Express the number 3.91×10^{-2} in standard form.

11. Express the number 0.00000005864 in scientific notation.

12. Express the number 3.92×10^{-6} in standard form.

13. **Higher Order Thinking** Express the mass 6,200,000 kilograms using scientific notation in kilograms, and then in grams.

✅ Assessment Practice

14. Which of the following numbers are written in scientific notation? Select all that apply.

- ☐ 34.2×10^9
- ☐ 1.80×10^9
- ☐ 19.9×10^9
- ☐ 5.99×10^{-9}
- ☐ 3.42×10^{-9}
- ☐ 18.0×10^{-9}

15. After evaluating an expression, your calculator display shows the result 4.5E−11.

PART A

Express this number in scientific notation.

PART B

Express this number in standard form.

Name: _____

1-10 Additional Practice

Leveled Practice In **1** and **2**, complete the expressions to find the answer.

1. Simplify the expression $(9.6 \times 10^{-8}) \div (2 \times 10^{-15})$. Express your answer in scientific notation.

$$\left(\boxed{} \div \boxed{} \right) \times \left(10^{\boxed{}} \div 10^{\boxed{}} \right)$$

$$\boxed{} \times 10^{\boxed{}}$$

2. Simplify the expression $(6.8 \times 10^6) + (3.4 \times 10^6)$. Express your answer in scientific notation.

$$\left(\boxed{} + \boxed{} \right) \times 10^{\boxed{}}$$

$$\boxed{} \times 10^{\boxed{}}$$

$$\boxed{} \times 10^{\boxed{}}$$

3. What is the value of n in the equation $2.6 \times 10^{-2} = (5.2 \times 10^7) \div (2 \times 10^n)$?

4. Simplify $(14.1 \times 10^5) - (2.9 \times 10^5)$. Write your answer in scientific notation.

5. What is the mass of 75,000 oxygen molecules? Express your answer in scientific notation.

Mass of one molecule of oxygen = 5.3×10^{-23} gram

6. **Critique Reasoning** Your friend says that the quotient of 9.2×10^8 and 4×10^{-3} is 2.4×10^5. Is this answer correct? Explain.

7. Find $(3.8 \times 10^7) \times 162$. Write your answer in scientific notation.

8. Find $\dfrac{10.5 \times 10^{-5}}{2.5 \times 10^{-2}}$. Write your answer in scientific notation.

9. Find $\frac{6.5 \times 10^{11}}{1.3 \times 10^8}$. Write your answer in scientific notation.

10. Find $(7.6 \times 10^3) \times (5.9 \times 10^{12})$. Write your answer in scientific notation.

11. The average U.S. resident uses 100 gallons of water per day. The population of the United States is about 3.23×10^8. About how many gallons of water do U.S. residents use each day? Express your answer in scientific notation.

12. **Higher Order Thinking**

   a. What is the value of n in the equation $1.8 \times 10^n = (6 \times 10^8)(3 \times 10^6)$

   b. Explain why the exponent on the left side of the equation is not equal to the sum of the exponents on the right side.

☑ Assessment Practice

13. Find $(4.54 \times 10^8) - (3.98 \times 10^8)$. When you regroup the decimals, what do you notice about their difference? How does this affect the exponent of the difference?

14. Which expression has the greatest value?

   Ⓐ $(3.23 \times 10^4) + (5.6 \times 10^{-3})$

   Ⓑ $(3.23 \times 10^4) - (5.6 \times 10^{-3})$

   Ⓒ $(3.23 \times 10^4) \times (5.6 \times 10^{-3})$

   Ⓓ $(3.23 \times 10^4) \div (5.6 \times 10^{-3})$

Name: _____

2-1 Additional Practice

Leveled Practice In **1** and **2**, complete the steps to solve for *x*.

1. $\frac{4}{7}x + \frac{5}{14}x = 39$

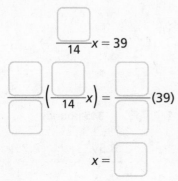

$\dfrac{\boxed{}}{14}x = 39$

$\dfrac{\boxed{}}{\boxed{}}\left(\dfrac{\boxed{}}{14}x\right) = \dfrac{\boxed{}}{\boxed{}}(39)$

$x = \boxed{}$

2. $-12.6x - 4.9x = -154$

$\boxed{}\,x = -154$

$x = \dfrac{-154}{\boxed{}}$

$x = \boxed{}$

In **3–6**, solve for *x*.

3. $2.4x - 9.1x + 12.5x = -39.44$

4. $-\frac{5}{6}x - \frac{1}{9}x = -102$

5. $\frac{5}{11}x + \frac{2}{3}x - \frac{1}{6}x = -189$

6. $8.7x - 1.9x = 116.96$

7. **Make Sense and Persevere** Wayne bought blueberries. He uses $\frac{3}{8}$ of the blueberries to make blueberry bread, $\frac{1}{6}$ of the blueberries to make pancakes, and $\frac{5}{12}$ of the blueberries to make jam. If Wayne uses 69 ounces of the blueberries he bought, how many ounces of blueberries did he buy?

8. **Make Sense and Persevere** Charlotte buys a ticket to go to a baseball game. The total includes a charge of 7% of the original price for extra fees. If Charlotte pays a total of $44.94, how much was the original price of the ticket?

9. Manuel bought 9 pounds of apples. He has eaten $\frac{3}{4}$ of a pound so far and has $15 worth of apples left. Write and solve an equation to find the cost of the apples per pound to the nearest dollar. How much did the apples cost per pound?

10. **Higher Order Thinking** Solve $\frac{3}{4}h - 12 = 8\frac{5}{8}$.

11. Timothy bought concrete mix for several projects. He used 3.5 bags of concrete mix for a new set of stairs and 2.25 bags of concrete mix for a garden wall. Timothy mixed 345 pounds of concrete in all.

345 pounds	
3.5y	2.25y

a. **Model with Math** Write an equation that can be represented by the bar diagram.

b. Solve for y. How many pounds of concrete does each bag make?

12. The community center has a pottery class each month. Each student pays $15 for the class and $27 for materials. This month the pottery class brought in a total of $714. How many students are in the class this month?

✓ Assessment Practice

13. **Construct Arguments** Your friend incorrectly says the solution to the equation $11.2y - 7.4y = 141.36$ is $y = 7.6$. What error did your friend make?

Ⓐ Divided incorrectly

Ⓑ Added $7.4y + 11.2y$

Ⓒ Solved for $\frac{1}{y}$ instead of y

Ⓓ Subtracted like terms incorrectly

14. Brian scored $\frac{1}{10}$ of the points for his basketball team in the state championship game. Joe scored $\frac{1}{4}$ of the points. Together they scored 21 points. Write an equation to represent the situation. What was the total number of points the team scored?

2-2 Additional Practice

Scan for Multimedia

Leveled Practice In **1** and **2**, solve each equation.

1. $6.4n - 10 = 4.4n + 6$

$$\boxed{}\, n - 10 = \boxed{}$$

$$\boxed{}\, n = \boxed{}$$

$$n = \boxed{}$$

2. $\frac{1}{3}k + 80 = \frac{1}{2}k + 120$

$$\frac{\boxed{}}{6}k + 80 = \frac{\boxed{}}{6}k + 120$$

$$\boxed{} = \frac{\boxed{}}{6}k + 120$$

$$\boxed{} = \frac{\boxed{}}{6}k$$

$$\boxed{} = k$$

3. You and a friend are doing math homework together. You have to solve the equation $5x + 4x - 68 = 34 - 8x$. Your friend arrives at the answer $x = -2$. Is she correct? Explain.

In **4** and **5**, solve the equation for x.

4. $\frac{5}{8}x + 4 = \frac{3}{8}x + 12$

5. $150 - x - 2x = 120 + 2x$

6. A rental car agency charges $240 per week plus $0.25 per mile to rent a car. The charge for a minivan is $180 per week plus $0.40 per mile. After how many miles is the total charge for each vehicle the same?

7. The Smith family and the Jackson family are having their basements remodeled. The Smith's contractor charges $16.50 per hour plus $289 in supplies. The Jackson's contractor charges $18.75 per hour and $274.60 in supplies. At how many hours of work will the total cost be the same for both families?

8. Jim currently has $1,250 in his bank account and Sally has $1,400 in her bank account. Jim deposits $27.50 per week and Sally deposits $20 per week into her account. After how many weeks will they have the same amount of money?

9. **Higher Order Thinking** The price of Stock A at 9 A.M. was $15.75. Since then, the price has been increasing at the rate of $0.05 per hour. At noon, the price of Stock B was $16.53. It begins to decrease at the rate of $0.13 per hour. If the stocks continue to increase and decrease at the same rates, in how many hours will the prices of the stocks be the same?

☑ Assessment Practice

10. Solve the equation $\frac{7}{3}x + \frac{1}{3}x = 1 + \frac{5}{3}x$. Show your work.

11. Schools A and B are competing in an academic contest. At the beginning of the final round, School A has 174 points and School B has 102 points. In the final round, correct answers earn 10 points and incorrect answers lose 6 points. School A gives the same number of correct and incorrect answers during the final round. School B gives no incorrect answers and the same number of correct answers as School A. The contest ends with the two schools tied.

PART A

Which equation models the scoring in the final round and the outcome of the contest?

Ⓐ $174 + 10x = 102 + 10x - 6x$

Ⓑ $174 + 10x - 6x = 102 + 4x$

Ⓒ $174 - 6x = 102 + 10x$

Ⓓ $174 + 10x - 6x = 102 + 10x$

PART B

How many correct answers does each school give during the final round?

PRACTICE TUTORIAL

2-3 Additional Practice

Scan for Multimedia

Leveled Practice In 1–3, find the value of x.

1. Donavon and three friends go to a fair. They each spend $\frac{1}{2}$ of their money on rides. Then they each spend $3 on food. At the end of the day, Donavon and his friends have a total of $8 remaining. How much money did each person bring to the fair?

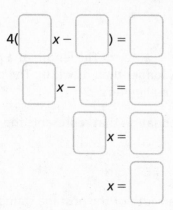

$$4(\boxed{}\,x - \boxed{}) = \boxed{}$$

$$\boxed{}\,x - \boxed{} = \boxed{}$$

$$\boxed{}\,x = \boxed{}$$

$$x = \boxed{}$$

Donavon and his friends each brought a total of $\boxed{}$.

2. Use the Distributive Property to solve the equation $25 - (3x + 5) = 2(x + 8) + x$.

$$25 - \boxed{}\,x - \boxed{} = 2x + \boxed{} + x$$

$$20 - \boxed{}\,x = \boxed{}\,x + \boxed{}$$

$$20 - \boxed{}\,x = \boxed{}$$

$$\boxed{}\,x = \boxed{}$$

$$x = \boxed{}$$

3. Use the Distributive Property to solve the equation $2(x - 3) + 3 = 6x - 5$.

$$\boxed{}\,x - \boxed{} + 3 = 6x - \boxed{}$$

$$\boxed{}\,x - \boxed{} = 6x - \boxed{}$$

$$\boxed{}\,x - \boxed{} = \boxed{}$$

$$\boxed{}\,x = \boxed{}$$

$$x = \boxed{}$$

4. Solve the equation $\frac{1}{5}(x - 2) = \frac{1}{10}(x + 6)$.

5. Solve the equation $0.35(x + 4) = 0.25(x - 6)$.

6. If you take $-\frac{3}{10}$ of a number and add 1, you get 10. Let x represent the original number.

   a. Write an equation that represents the situation.

   b. What is the original number?

7. Solve the equation $-9(x + 6) = -207$.

8. Use the Distributive Property to solve the equation $5x - 3(x - 3) = -6 + 6x - 5$.

9. Higher Order Thinking The length of a postage stamp is $4\frac{1}{4}$ millimeters longer than its width. The perimeter of the stamp is $124\frac{1}{2}$ millimeters.

 a. Write the equation that represents the situation.

 b. What is the width of the postage stamp?

 c. What is the length of the postage stamp?

✅ Assessment Practice

10. You are given the equation $2(\frac{1}{2}t + 3) = 1$ to solve as part of a homework assignment.

PART A

Describe the first step needed to solve the equation.

PART B

Solve the equation for t. Show your work.

11. Solve the equation $2(6 - x) = 3(x - 1)$.

2-4 Additional Practice

1. **Leveled Practice** Classify the equation $6x + 4x - 1 = 2(5x + 4)$ as having one solution, infinitely many solutions, or no solution.

$6x + 4x - 1 = 2(5x + 4)$

$6x + 4x - 1 = \boxed{} \cdot 5x + \boxed{} \cdot 4$

$\boxed{} - 1 = \boxed{} + \boxed{}$

$10x - \boxed{} - 1 = 10x - \boxed{} + 8$

Since $-1 \boxed{}$ 8, the equation has $\boxed{}$ solution(s).

For 2–7, classify each equation as having one solution, no solution, or infinitely many solutions. If one solution, write the solution.

2. $48x + 43 = 47x + 43$

3. $2(3x + 8) = 2x + 16 + 4x$

4. $0.4(5x - 15) = 2.5(x + 3)$

5. $3(4x + 2) = 20x - 9x + 2$

6. $4(9x + 6) = 36x - 7$

7. $8(2x + 5) = 16x + 40$

8. Solve $4(2x + 3) = 16x + 3 - 8x + 9$.

9. Solve $8.2(6x - 3) = 7(7x - 1.2)$.

10. **Critique Reasoning** Your friend solved the equation
$4x + 24x - 2 = 7(4x + 2)$ and got $x = 16$. What error did your
friend make? What is the correct solution?

11. **Higher Order Thinking** Using the expression $x + 3$, write one
equation that has one solution, one equation that has no solution,
and one equation that has infinitely many solutions. Explain.

   a. one solution

   b. no solution

   c. infinitely many solutions

✔ Assessment Practice

12. Which of the following statements are true about the equation
$x + 4x + 4 = 3(2x - 1)$? Select all that apply.

   ☐ Operations that can be used to solve the equation are addition and multiplication.

   ☐ Operations that can be used to solve the equation are addition and division.

   ☐ The equation has infinitely many solutions.

   ☐ The equation has one solution, $x = 7$.

   ☐ The equation has two solutions, $x = 7$ and $x = -7$.

   ☐ The equation has no solution.

13. Two ice cream shops in the mall sell sundaes. Let x equal the number
of scoops of ice cream. Larry's Ice Cream Shop's price is represented by
the expression $1.2x + 1$. Ice Cream World's price is represented by the
expression $0.4(0.3x + 1)$. Which statement is true?

   Ⓐ The two shops charge the same price for a 3-scoop sundae.

   Ⓑ The two shops always charge the same price for sundaes with the same number of scoops.

   Ⓒ The two shops never charge the same price for sundaes with the same number of scoops.

   Ⓓ The two shops charge the same price for a 2-scoop sundae.

Name: _____

2-5 Additional Practice

Scan for Multimedia

1. Leveled Practice The graph and the table show the total cost of the number of pairs of jeans purchased at two different stores. Which store charges the higher cost for a pair of jeans?

Find the unit rate (constant of proportionality) for Jenny's Jean Store.

$$\frac{cost}{pairs} = \frac{\square}{\square} = \$\square \text{ per pair}$$

Find the unit rate (constant of proportionality) for Jean Warehouse.

$$\frac{cost}{pairs} = \frac{\square}{\square} = \$\square \text{ per pair}$$

So _____ charges the higher rate.

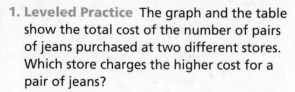

Jenny's Jean Store

Jean Warehouse				
Pairs of Jeans	2	3	4	5
Total Cost ($)	36	54	72	90

2. The graph shows the average speed of Car 1 which is traveling on a highway. The equation $y = 55x$ represents the average speed of Car 2, where y is the distance in miles and x is the time in hours. Which car is traveling at the greater speed?

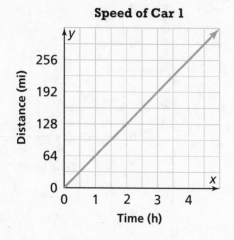

Speed of Car 1

3. The graph shows a proportional relationship between the number of workers and weekly cost, in dollars, for a company in its first year. The following year, the company spends $7,200 per 12 employees. Did the rate increase or decrease the following year?

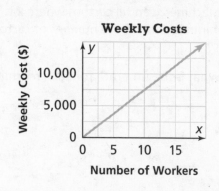

Weekly Costs

2-5 Compare Proportional Relationships **29**

4. Corey compares the heights of two plants to see which plant grows more per week. The table shows the relationship between the height and number of weeks for Plant 1. The graph shows the relationship between the height and number of weeks for Plant 2.

Which plant grows at the faster rate?

Plant 1

Weeks	2	3	4	5
Height (inches)	8	12	16	20

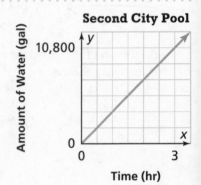

Plant 2

5. **Higher Order Thinking** At the beginning of summer, a maintenance crew refills a swimming pool at a city park. The relationship between the time in hours to fill the pool and the amount of water in the pool is proportional. After 4 hours, the pool holds 5,200 gallons of water.

   a. How could you graph this relationship?

Second City Pool

   b. The same crew refills a second pool as represented by the graph shown. Is the second pool filled at a faster or a slower rate than the first pool? Explain.

6. The graph shows the relationship between the time in minutes and the number of milk cartons that Machine 1 can fill. The equation $y = 22x$ describes the rate at which Machine 2 can fill cartons where x is the number of minutes and y is the number of cartons filled.

PART A

What is the unit rate for each machine?

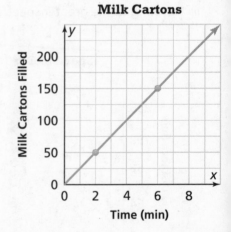

Milk Cartons

PART B

Which machine can fill cartons at a faster rate? How much faster?

Name: _____

2-6 Additional Practice

Scan for
Multimedia

Leveled Practice In **1 and 2**, find the slope of each line.

1. Find the slope of the line.

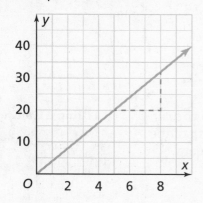

slope = $\frac{\text{rise}}{\text{run}}$

= $\frac{\Box}{\Box}$ = $\Box$

The slope is $\Box$.

2. Find the slope of the line. Use the two points shown.

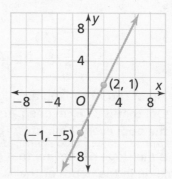

slope = $\frac{\text{rise}}{\text{run}}$

= $\frac{1 - \Box}{\Box - \Box}$

= $\frac{\Box}{\Box}$ = $\Box$

The slope is $\Box$.

For 3 and 4, find the slope of the line that passes through the given points.

3. (0, 10) and (24, 6)

4. (0, 6) and (20, 14)

---

5. The graph shows the number of centimeters a particular plant grows over time.

   a. What is the slope of the line?

   b. Reasoning What does the slope mean?

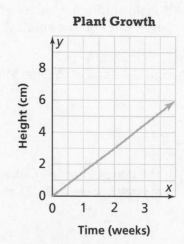

Plant Growth

---

6. A machinist measures the thickness of a grinding pad every week. The graph shows how many millimeters the grinding pad has worn down.

   a. What is the slope of the line?

   b. **Reasoning** What does the slope mean?

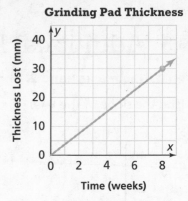
Grinding Pad Thickness

7. **Higher Order Thinking** You use a garden hose to fill a circular wading pool that is 83.6 cm deep. You measure the depth of the water in the pool every 2 minutes. The table shows the data.

   a. What is the slope of the line that represents the change in the depth of the water?

   b. What does this slope mean?

   c. How many minutes will it take to fill the pool?

Filling a Wading Pool

Time (minutes)	Depth of Water (cm)
0	0
2	4.4
4	8.8
6	13.2
8	17.6
10	22.0

8. The graph shows the number of kilometers Gina swims. What is the slope of the line and what does it mean?

Distance Swimming

☑ Assessment Practice

9. Donald graphs the distance he walks over time. The graph passes through the points (3, 12) and (4, 16).

   PART A

   Find the slope of the line that passes through these points.

   PART B

   Is the slope between (1, 4) and (3, 12) the same as the slope between (3, 12) and (4, 16)? Explain.

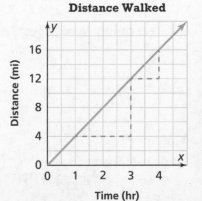
Distance Walked

2-7 Additional Practice

1. **Leveled Practice** The graph shows the number of possible passengers for a given number of roller coaster cars that leave the platform.

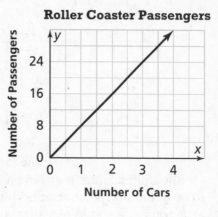

Roller Coaster Passengers

a. Use two sets of coordinates to write an equation to describe the relationship.

$$m = \frac{24 - \square}{\square - 2} = \frac{\square}{\square}$$

$$y = \boxed{}\,x$$

b. Interpret the equation in words.

Each roller coaster car holds $\boxed{}$ passengers.

2. **Model with Math** The graph relates the actual size of a car in feet to a model of the car in inches. Write an equation that describes the relationship.

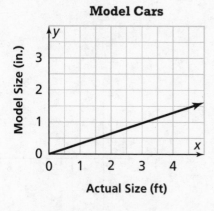

Model Cars

Model Size (in.)

Actual Size (ft)

3. Graph the equation $y = \frac{2}{3}x$ on the coordinate plane.

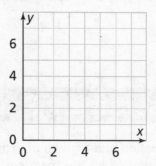

4. A park volunteer plans to work on the park's stone walls for 1 hour every Monday, 1 hour every Wednesday, and 3 hours on Fridays. The graph shows the number of hours he plans to work for a given number of weeks.

a. Find the constant of proportionality of the line. Then find the slope of the line.

b. Write an equation to describe the relationship.

c. How many hours will the volunteer work in 16 weeks?

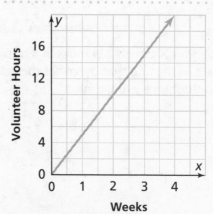

Volunteer Hours

Weeks

5. Model with Math Graph the equation $y = -10x$ on the coordinate plane.

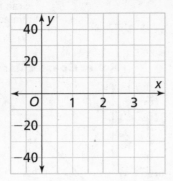

6. Write an equation in the form $y = mx$ for the proportional relationship that passes through the points $(2, -15)$ and $(6, -45)$.

7. Higher Order Thinking The longest aerial tramway in the United States is at Sandia Peak in New Mexico. The graph shows the relationship between the time of the tram ride and its elevation above the base.

a. Use the points $(5, 1{,}273)$ and $(10, 2{,}546)$ to write an equation for the line.

b. Interpret the equation in words.

c. Explain why the line is valid only for the first quadrant.

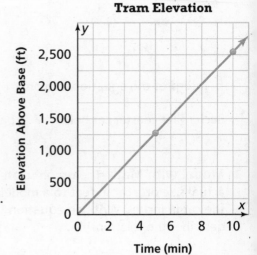

Tram Elevation

✓ Assessment Practice

8. An equation and a graph of proportional relationships are shown. Which has the greater unit rate?

$y = \frac{13}{2}x$

9. Bus X travels 224 miles in 4 hours. Write the equation of the line that describes the relationship between distance y and time x.

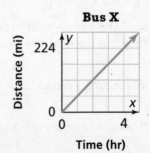

Bus X

PRACTICE   TUTORIAL

2-8 Additional Practice

Scan for
Multimedia

1. Leveled Practice Find the *y*-intercept for the line.

The *y*-intercept is the point where the graph crosses

the ⬚-axis.

The line crosses the *y*-axis at (⬚, ⬚).

So, the *y*-intercept is ⬚.

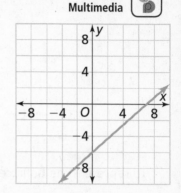

2. The line models the height of a glider *y*, in feet, over *x* hours.

a. Find the *y*-intercept of the graph.

b. What does the *y*-intercept represent?

Height of Glider

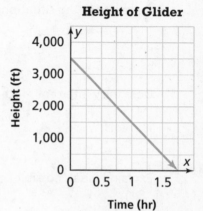

3. Which graph represents a proportional relationship? Explain.

Graph A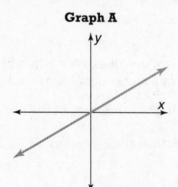

Graph B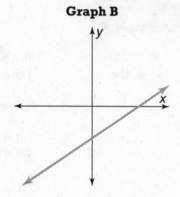

Graph C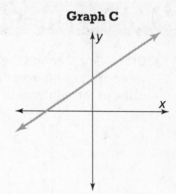

4. The line models the temperature starting at noon on an autumn day.

a. Find the *y*-intercept of the function.

b. What does the *y*-intercept represent?

**Temperature on
Autumn Day**

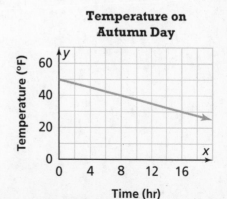

5. Which graph has a *y*-intercept of −5? Explain.

Graph A

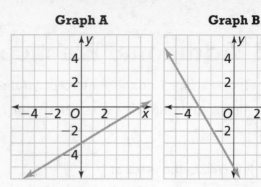

Graph B

6. **Higher Order Thinking** Tasha incorrectly draws this graph to represent the balance in her savings account over time.

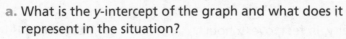
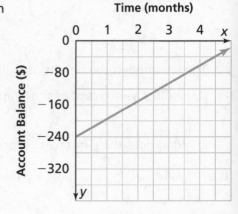

a. What is the *y*-intercept of the graph and what does it represent in the situation?

b. Does the *y*-intercept make sense in this situation? Explain.

c. Explain Tasha's possible error.

☑ Assessment Practice

7. Draw a line through the point such that the value of the *y*-intercept is the same as the value of the *x*-intercept.

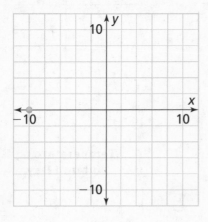

8. Which statement describes the *y*-intercept of the graph of a proportional relationship?

Ⓐ It is equal to the *x*-intercept of the line.

Ⓑ It is greater than the *x*-intercept of the line.

Ⓒ The line intersects the *y*-axis of the graph at the origin.

Ⓓ The line intersects the *y*-axis of the graph above the origin.

Name: _____

2-9 Additional Practice

1. Leveled Practice What is the graph of the equation $y = -\frac{1}{4}x + 2$?

The *y*-intercept is ☐ , which means the line crosses the *y*-axis

at the point (☐ , ☐). Plot this point.

The slope of the line is negative, so it goes ☐ from left to right.

Start at the *y*-intercept. Move down ☐ , and then move right

☐ . You are now at the point (☐ , ☐). Plot this point.

Draw a line to connect the two points.

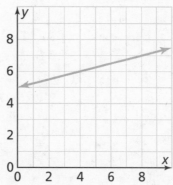

---

2. Write an equation for the line in slope-intercept form.

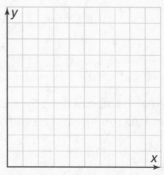

---

3. Danny is opening a savings account with an initial deposit of $45. He saves $3 per day.

a. Draw a line to show the relationship between the number of days, *x*, and the total amount in his account, *y*.

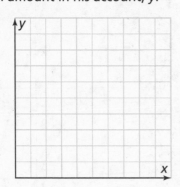

b. What is the equation of the line in slope-intercept form?

4. Linnea is renting a bike. It costs $4.50 per hour plus a $5 deposit.

a. Draw a line to show the relationship between the number of hours a bike is rented, *x*, and the total cost of renting a bike, *y*.

b. What is the equation of the line in slope-intercept form?

5. The line models a recipe for chicken pie. The recipe calls for 14 ounces of chicken for the first 4 people. The recipe calls for 6 ounces of chicken for each additional person.

   a. Write an equation for the line in slope-intercept form, where x is the number of additional people and y is the total number of ounces.

   b. If you have 26 ounces of chicken, how many people can you feed?

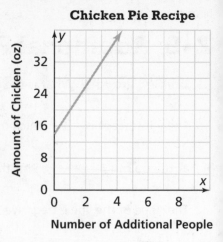

Chicken Pie Recipe

Amount of Chicken (oz)

Number of Additional People

6. **Higher Order Thinking** You are given the equation $y - 8 = \frac{3}{5}(x - 5)$ as part of your homework assignment.

   a. Write this equation in slope-intercept form.

   b. Graph the equation.

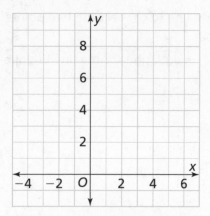

✓ Assessment Practice

7. Write an equation in slope-intercept form for each line at the right.

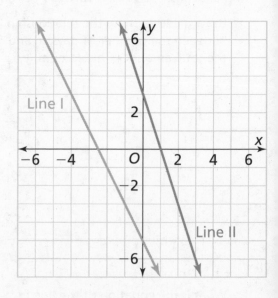

Line I

Line II

8. What is the equation $5y + 22 = 5x - 33$ written in slope intercept form?

   Ⓐ $y = x - 11$

   Ⓑ $y = 5x - 55$

   Ⓒ $5x = 5y + 55$

   Ⓓ $x = y + 11$

3-1 Additional Practice

Scan for
Multimedia

1. The set of ordered pairs (1, 7), (3, 8), (3, 6), (6, 5), (2, 11), (1, 4) represents a relation.

    a. Make an arrow diagram that represents the relation.

    b. Is the relation a function? Explain.

2. Is the relation shown in the table a function? Explain.

Input	Output
1	3
2	6
3	9
4	12

3. The relation shown below represents the temperature, in degrees Celsius, of the air a certain number of hours after noon on a winter day. Is the temperature a function of time? Explain.

(2, −1), (1, −6), (6, −3), (4, −7)

4. Make an arrow diagram to represent the relation shown in the table. Is the relation a function? Explain.

Input	Output
1	2
11	32
15	2
16	32

5. Construct Arguments The set of ordered pairs (1, 8.50), (3, 25.50), (5, 42.50), (6, 51), (7, 59.50) represents the cost of tickets for the school play for different numbers of tickets. The input represents the number of tickets, and the output represents the total cost. Is the cost a function of the number of tickets? Explain.

6. a. **Use Structure** How can an arrow diagram help to determine whether a relation is a function?

b. Make an arrow diagram that describes the relation (3, 39), (6, 39), (9, 78), (15, 117).

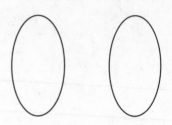

7. **Higher Order Thinking** Jan made the arrow diagram below to determine whether the relation shown in the table represents a function. She determines that the relation is not a function. Is Jan's answer correct? Explain your response.

Input	Output
−3	−24
2	−42
12	−24
14	−42

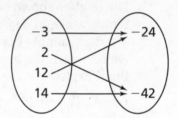

☑ Assessment Practice

8. Is the set of ordered pairs presented in the arrow diagram a function? Explain.

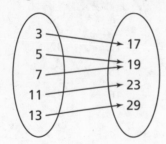

9. Which of these relations are functions? Select all that apply.

☐ (4, 4), (5, 6), (6, 8), (6, 10), (7, 12)

☐ (6, 9), (7, 19), (8, 29), (8, 39), (9, 49)

☐ (4, 4), (5, 4), (6, 4), (7, 4), (8, 4)

☐ (7, 33), (8, 30), (9, 27), (10, 24), (11, 21)

☐ (1, 2), (2, 2), (2, −2), (3, −2), (4, −2)

Name: _____

3-2 Additional Practice

Scan for Multimedia

In **1** and **2**, explain whether the graph represents a function.

1.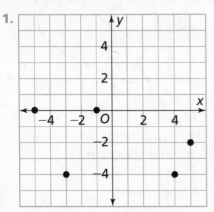

2.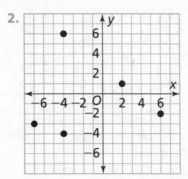

3. Marcus records the total number of Calories burned after each mile he walks.

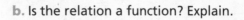

Miles Walked (x)	1	2	3
Calories Burned (y)	97	194	291

a. Graph the ordered pairs from the table.

b. Is the relation a function? Explain.

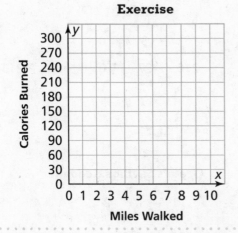

4. The relationship between the amount of powdered fertilizer, x, needed to make y gallons of liquid fertilizer is shown in the table. Is the relation a function? Use the graph to support your answer.

x	0	6	12	18
y	0	4	8	12

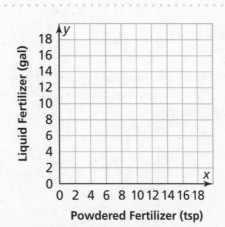

3-2 Connect Representations of Functions   41

5. Robert swims a lap in the pool. His coach graphs his distance from the starting block.

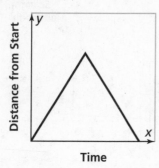 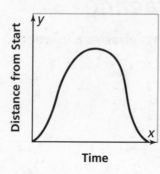 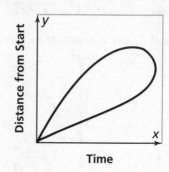

a. Determine whether each graph is a function. Justify your answer.

b. **Construct Arguments** Which graph must be incorrect? Explain.

6. **Higher Order Thinking** Which of these tables represent a nonlinear function?

Table I

Input	3	6	9	12	15
Output	1	4	9	16	25

Table II

Input	2	4	6	8	10
Output	19	9	−1	−11	−21

Table III

Input	6	3	0	−3	−6
Output	216	27	0	−27	−216

☑ Assessment Practice

7. Greta opens a savings account with $25. She saves $20 each week. The table represents her account balance.

Greta's Savings Account

Week	0	1	2	3	4	5
Money in Account	25	45	65	85	105	125

PART A

Write a function that reiates the amount of money in Greta's account, *m*, to the number of weeks, *w*.

PART B

Is the relation a linear or a nonlinear function? Explain.

PRACTICE   TUTORIAL

3-3 Additional Practice

Scan for
Multimedia

1. Two linear functions are shown below. Which function has the greater rate of change?

Function A

x	y
4	32
8	44
12	56
16	68
20	80

Function B

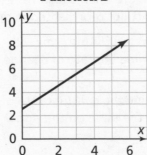

2. Two linear functions are shown below. Which function has the greater initial value?

Function A

$y = \frac{3}{4}x + 5$

Function B

x	−2	0	2	4	6
y	5	8	11	14	17

3. Tell whether each function is *linear* or *nonlinear*.

Function A

x	−2	1	2	3	4
y	3	0	−1	−2	−3

Function B

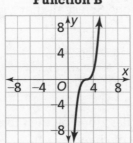

4. Decide whether each function is *linear* or *nonlinear* from its graph.

Function I

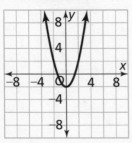

Function II

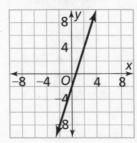

Function III

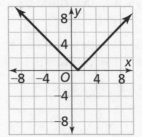

5. **Look for Relationships** Which two functions have the same rate of change?

   A. $y = 0.5x - 1$ B. $y = 4x - 7$ C. $n = 0.6r + 1$ D. $t = 0.5n + 1$

6. **Make Sense and Persevere** Glen compares the rates of change of two linear functions represented in different forms.

   a. For a linear function in the form $y = mx + b$, how does Glen determine the rate of change?

   b. How can Glen determine the constant rate of change of the linear function presented in the table on the right? What is the rate of change?

x	y
1	22
2	20
3	18
4	16

7. **Critique Reasoning** The table on the right and the equation $y = 8x + 5$ describe linear functions. A student states incorrectly that the initial values of the functions are equal. Compare the initial values of the functions. What mistake did the student likely make?

x	y
0	8
1	9
2	10
3	11

✅ Assessment Practice

8. The equation $y = 4x + 60$ and the table each describe a linear function. Compare the properties of the functions. Select all that apply.

x	10	20	30	40
y	60	80	100	120

   ☐ The linear function described by the table has the greater rate of change.

   ☐ The linear function described by the equation has the greater rate of change.

   ☐ The rates of change are equal.

   ☐ The linear function described by the table has the greater initial value.

   ☐ The linear function described by the equation has the greater initial value.

   ☐ The initial values are equal.

9. Jeff saved $500 from his summer job so he would have spending money during the school year. He withdraws $12 from his account each week, so a linear function models his plan. Melissa made a similar plan. The table shows the results of her first five transactions. Compare the functions.

   Melissa's Savings

Week	1	2	3	4	5
Balance	$510	$500	$490	$480	$470

Name: _____

3-4 Additional Practice

Scan for
Multimedia

In 1–4, answer the questions related to the following situation.

The graph models the depth of the water in a small fountain during a rainstorm.

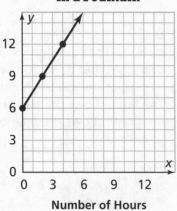

**The Depth of Water
in a Fountain**

1. What is the y-intercept?

2. What does the y-intercept represent?

3. What does the slope represent?

4. Write a linear function in the form $y = mx + b$ for this line.

5. The graph shows the outdoor temperature on a certain winter day starting at sunrise.

   a. What do the slope and y-intercept of this function represent?

   b. Write a linear function in the form $y = mx + b$ for this line.

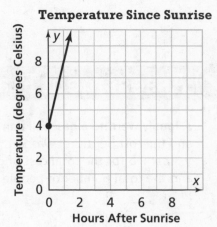

Temperature Since Sunrise

For 6–7, write the equation that models each linear relationship.

6.

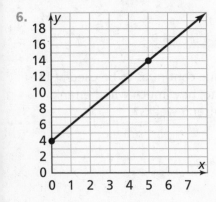

7.

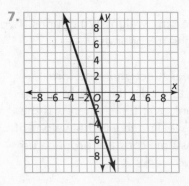

8. Carla is saving money for a trip this summer. She already has some money in her savings account and will add the same amount to her account each week. At the end of 2 weeks, Carla has $130. At the end of 8 weeks, she has $280. Write a linear function in the form $y = mx + b$ to represent the amount of money, m, that Carla has saved after w weeks.

9. **Higher Order Thinking** Stations 1, 2, and 3 are bus stations. The equation $y = 160x$ represents the number of people that go to Station 1, where y is the total number of people and x is the number of hours since opening. The table shows the same relationship for Station 2, and the graph shows the relationship for Station 3.

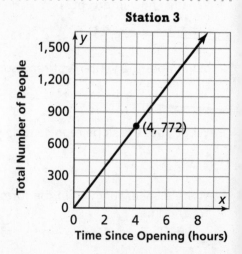

Station 3

Station 2

Hours Since Opening, x	2	3	4	5
Total Number of People, y	326	489	652	815

a. Which station has the greatest number of people arrive per hour?

b. What is the total number of people who have gone to a bus station after 4 hours?

10. A family went to a baseball game. The cost to park the car was $5 and the cost per ticket was $21. Write a linear function in the form $y = mx + b$ for the total cost of going to the baseball game, y, and the total number of people in the family, x.

11. A full propane tank weighs 170 pounds. Two weeks later, the tank weighs 165 pounds.

a. Write a linear function in the form $y = mx + b$ to model the weight of the propane tank over time, where x is the number of weeks and y is the weight of the tank. Assume constant propane use over the two weeks.

b. If propane continues to be used at the same rate, how much will the tank weigh after 5 weeks?

3-5 Additional Practice

Scan for
Multimedia
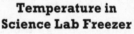

1. Leveled Practice Use the graph to complete the statements.

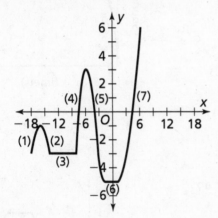

2. The graph below shows the temperature inside a freezer in a science lab. Is the function increasing, decreasing, or constant? Explain.

**Temperature in
Science Lab Freezer**

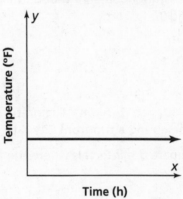

The function is ☐ in intervals 2 and 5.

The function is ☐ in intervals 1, 4, and 7.

The function is ☐ in intervals 3 and 6.

3. Make Sense and Persevere Demi went for a run in the park. The graph shows her speed during the run.

a. Describe the graph when the function is decreasing.

b. In how many intervals is the function decreasing?

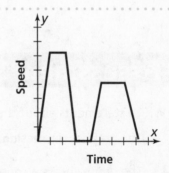

In 4–5, determine the intervals in which the function is increasing, decreasing, or constant.

4.

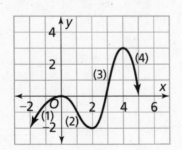

5.

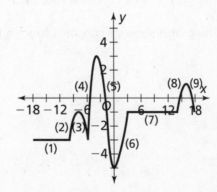

6. You have a device that monitors the sound level of a conversation located 1 meter away. The results are shown in the graph.

   a. Describe the relationship of the sound level as a function of time.

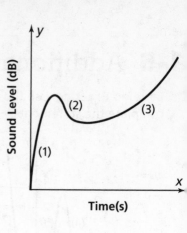

   b. **Reasoning** Compare the sound level during Intervals 1 and 3.

7. **Higher Order Thinking** The graph shows the speed of an airplane during a trip from City X to City Z.

   a. Compare the intervals where the function is increasing.

   b. Compare the intervals where the function is decreasing.

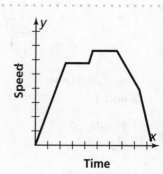

Assessment Practice

8. Which statements about the graph are true? Select all that apply.

   ☐ The graph is decreasing in intervals (1) and (4).

   ☐ The graph shows a constant function in interval (1).

   ☐ The graph is increasing in intervals (2) and (4).

   ☐ The graph has a constant rate of change.

   ☐ The graph shows a constant function in interval (3).

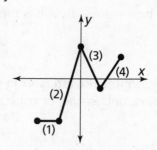

Name: _____

PRACTICE   TUTORIAL

Scan for Multimedia

1. An airplane ascends for 20 minutes. It flies at its cruising altitude for an hour. Then it descends for 15 minutes. Which graph shows the relationship between the time in flight and the altitude of the airplane?

Ⓐ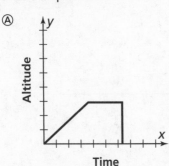

Ⓑ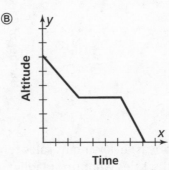

Ⓒ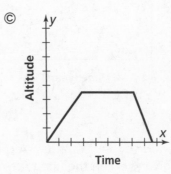

2. Which of the following descriptions best matches the graph below?

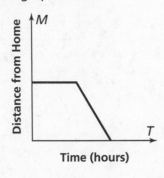

Ⓐ Gail is at a friend's house for a few hours. She then walks home.

Ⓑ Gail is at her house. She then walks to her friend's house.

Ⓒ Gail is at her house and does not leave.

Ⓓ Gail is at a friend's house for a few hours. She then walks to another friend's house farther away from her home.

3. Write a situation to match the given graph.

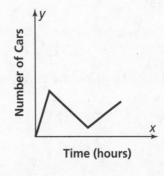

4. On a given day, the outdoor temperature was cool in the early morning and then rose steadily until noon. From noon until late afternoon, the temperature remained constant. The temperature dropped steadily for a few hours and then remained constant. Sketch a qualitative graph that represents the relationship between the time and the temperature.

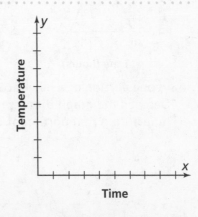

5. Write a situation to match the graph.

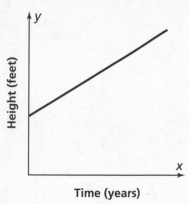

Height (feet) vs Time (years)

6. Look for Relationships As the price of a certain car increases, fewer cars are sold. Sketch a graph that shows the relationship between the price of the car and the number of cars sold.

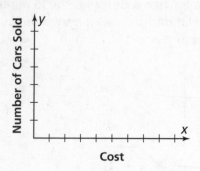

Number of Cars Sold vs Cost

7. Higher Order Thinking A company is reviewing its sales for a given year. In the first two months, sales went up steadily every month. Over the next four months, sales declined steadily. In the next three months, sales remained constant and then increased steadily during the last three months of the year.

a. Sketch a graph that shows the relationship between time and sales.

b. What might explain the behavior of the sales for the company?

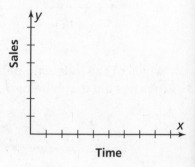

Sales vs Time

Assessment Practice

8. You bike 6.5 miles from home to a friend's house. On the way you stop at a store that is 2.25 miles from home. You bike at a speed of 7 miles per hour. Which graph describes the total distance you biked?

Ⓐ
Biking Trip
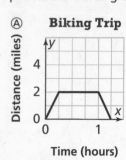
Distance (miles) vs Time (hours)

Ⓑ
Biking Trip
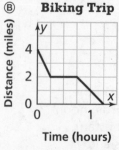
Distance (miles) vs Time (hours)

Ⓒ
Biking Trip
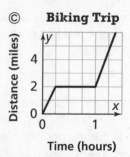
Distance (miles) vs Time (hours)

Ⓓ
Biking Trip
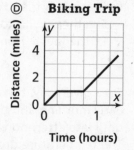
Distance (miles) vs Time (hours)

9. In one portion of a bike race Marco bikes at a constant speed of 9 miles per hour. Describe the graph that represents the relationship between Marco's distance and time during that portion of the race.

Name: _____

4-1 Additional Practice

1. Leveled Practice The table shows the year and the average price for one gallon of gasoline at a certain gas station. Complete the scatter plot.

Gasoline Prices

Year	2002	2003	2004	2005	2006	2007	2008	2009
Price ($)	1.32	1.53	1.81	2.28	2.58	2.82	3.24	2.32

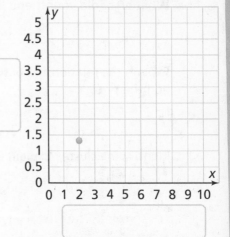

Gasoline Prices

2. The table shows the number of people and the total cost of their movie tickets at various movie theaters.

Theater Prices

Number of People	Total Cost ($)
2	15.00
3	13.50
3	22.50
4	18.00
5	37.50

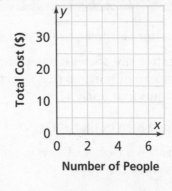

Theater Prices

a. Complete the scatter plot to represent the data.

b. Identify any outliers in the scatter plot. What situation might have caused an outlier?

3. Model with Math The scatter plot represents the numbers of hours since the city parking lots opened and the number of cars in the parking lots.

a. Identify any outliers in the scatter plot.

b. Identify any clusters in the scatter plot.

c. Identify any gaps in the scatter plot. What situation might have caused the gap?

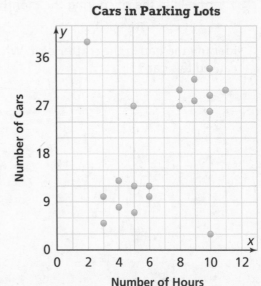

Cars in Parking Lots

4. Higher Order Thinking The scatter plot represents the price and the number of items sold. Your friend incorrectly says that the cluster in the graph is between the prices of $3 and $25 and between 5 and 20 items sold.

Items Sold

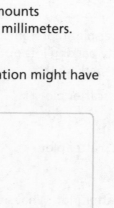

a. What error did your friend likely make?

b. Explain the relationship between the number of items sold and the price.

c. Identify the cluster. Explain what it tells you about the data.

✓ Assessment Practice

Use the scatter plot to answer 5 and 6.

5. The scatter plot shows the day of a month and the amount of rain in a city. Select all statements that apply.

☐ There is an outlier at Day 26.

☐ There is a cluster of days when it rained between Days 6 and 15.

☐ There is a gap of no rain falling between Days 10 and 26.

☐ There were three days of the month when it rained exactly 27 millimeters.

☐ The greatest difference in the recorded amounts of rain in the city during the month was 3 millimeters.

Rainfall

6. Identify the gap in the scatter plot. What situation might have caused this gap?

Name: _____

1. Which line is the best model of the data?

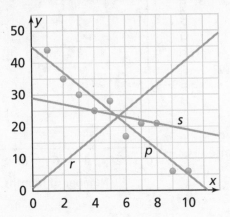

2. Does the scatter plot show a positive, a negative, or no association?

In 3 and 4, determine whether the scatter plot of the data for the situation given would have a positive or negative linear association.

3. Age of a car and reliability of a car

4. Treadmill running time and calories burned

5. Describe the relationship between the data in the scatter plot.

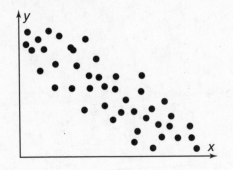

6. Describe the relationship between the data in the scatter plot.

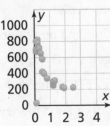

7. **Higher Order Thinking** A business manager was hired 9 months ago and wants a raise. The scatter plot shows the number of new customers that the manager brought to the company.

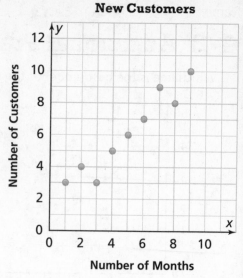

New Customers

a. Draw a trend line for the scatter plot.

b. What type of association does the scatter plot show?

c. Use the information from the scatter plot to explain why the manager should or should not receive a raise.

8. Describe a real situation that will show a negative linear association.

9. Which paired data are likely to show a nonlinear association? Select all that apply.

- ☐ Age and number of siblings
- ☐ Amount of money earned and length of hair
- ☐ Area and side length of a square
- ☐ Age and weight of puppies
- ☐ Height of a bouncing ball and time

10. Which paired data would likely show a positive association? Select all that apply.

- ☐ Population and number of supermarkets
- ☐ Time spent watching TV and grades on math tests
- ☐ Time spent studying and grades on math tests
- ☐ Hours worked and money earned
- ☐ Hours worked and hair length

PRACTICE
 TUTORIAL

4-3 Additional Practice

Scan for
Multimedia

1. Leveled Practice The scatter plot shows Leanna's elevation
above sea level during a hike. The trend line passes through
the points (30, 1070) and (75, 1680). If Leanna starts at
663 feet above sea level and maintains the same rate,
how far above sea level will she be after one hour?

The y-intercept is [ ].

The slope is [ ] = [ ].

The equation for the trend line is

y = [ ] x + [ ].

After one hour, her altitude will be

[ ] ([ ]) + [ ] = [ ]

feet above sea level.

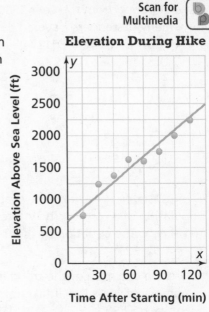

Elevation During Hike

y-axis: Elevation Above Sea Level (ft): 0, 500, 1000, 1500, 2000, 2500, 3000

x-axis: Time After Starting (min): 0, 30, 60, 90, 120

2. Make Sense and Persevere The scatter plot shows
the annual profit for one airline. The equation of the
trend line shown is $y = 0.4x + 4.1$, where x represents
the number of years since 2000 and y represents
the revenue in millions of dollars. What was the
approximate difference in revenue between
2003 and 2007?

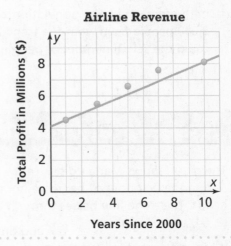

Airline Revenue

y-axis: Total Profit in Millions ($): 0, 2, 4, 6, 8

x-axis: Years Since 2000: 0, 2, 4, 6, 8, 10

3. An arctic cold front is moving through an area. It is 37°
when the temperature begins to drop. The scatter plot
suggests a linear relationship between the temperature
and the number of hours since the cold front arrived.

a. What does the rate of change, or slope, represent in
this situation?

b. What is the y-intercept for the trend line and what
does it represent?

c. What equation relates the change in temperature, y,
to the number of hours after the cold front arrives, x?

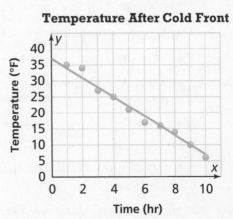

Temperature After Cold Front

y-axis: Temperature (°F): 0, 5, 10, 15, 20, 25, 30, 35, 40

x-axis: Time (hr): 0, 2, 4, 6, 8, 10

4. The scatter plot shows the number of passengers at a major airport over a 15-year period from the year 2000. About how many passengers traveled through this airport in the year 2011?

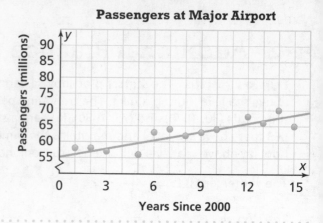

Passengers at Major Airport

5. **Higher Order Thinking** The graph shows the population of a certain city, y, over the course of 10 years, x. The equation of the trend line shown is $y = 1.9x + 21$.

   a. Use the equation of the trend line to predict the number of years it will take for the population to reach 52,900.

   b. In the tenth year, the population was actually 2,000 people from what the trend line shows. What could the actual number of people be in 10 years?

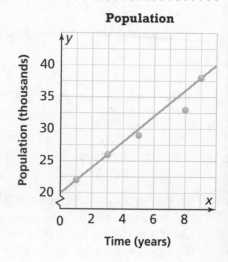

Population

✅ Assessment Practice

6. The graph shows Maria's distance from her house during the first hour of her drive home from the beach. The trend line passes through the points (0, 94) and (30, 70).

   Which statements about the graph are true?

   ☐ The data show a negative correlation.

   ☐ The trend line is $y = -\frac{4}{5}x + 94$.

   ☐ In general, Maria's distance from home is decreasing.

   ☐ Maria started her drive about 85 miles from home.

   ☐ After 30 minutes, Maria was about 60 miles from home

   ☐ After 60 minutes, Maria was home.

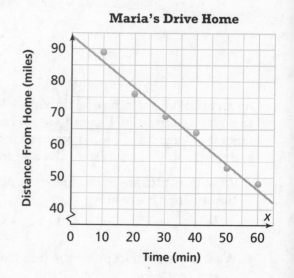

Maria's Drive Home

4-4 Additional Practice

Scan for Multimedia

1. Leveled Practice You ask 170 of your classmates how often they send a letter in the mail. Complete the two-way frequency table to show the results of the survey.

		Frequency				
		Weekly	Monthly	Yearly	Never	Total
Gender	Girls	☐	20	15	☐	90
	Boys	15	10	☐	☐	☐
	Total	40	☐	40	60	170

2. Make Sense and Persevere
A television broadcasting company asked a sample of its customers, "What type of program do you watch most frequently?" The two-way frequency table shows the results of the survey. If the company wants to decrease the number of programs offered, which type of program should it choose to cut? Explain.

Television Programs

		Type of Program				
		Comedy	Drama	Sports	News	Total
Gender	Women	123	215	89	306	733
	Men	127	110	217	222	676
	Total	250	325	306	528	1,409

3. A new radio station wants to know which type of music people in the area like the most. The station took a survey and displayed the results in a two-way frequency table.

a. If the radio station wants to mainly play two of the categories, which two categories would result in the most listeners? Explain.

Survey Results

		Gender		
		Women	Men	Total
Type of Music	Pop	35	42	77
	Rock	61	46	107
	Jazz	52	43	95
	Country	44	41	85
	Alternative	36	53	89
	Total	228	225	453

b. Which two categories draw about the same number of women and men? Explain.

4. **Higher Order Thinking** You ask 100 of your classmates if they like winter. There are 15 girls who like winter, 25 who do not, and 5 with no opinion. There are 20 boys who like winter, 10 who do not, and 25 with no opinion.

a. Construct a two-way frequency table to show the results of the survey.

Like Winter?		Gender		
		Girls	Boys	Total
	Yes			
	No			
	No Opinion			
	Total			

b. Does one group like winter more than the other? Explain.

c. Why might an opinion made based on this data be incorrect?

5. A researcher tracks data about the outgoing mail in a large office.

PART A
Complete the two-way frequency table to show the researcher's results.

Type		Type of Delivery		
		Regular	Overnight	Total
	Letter		5	
	Package	25		35
	Total			55

PART B
Which type of outgoing mail is delivered from the office less frequently? Explain.

Name: _____

4-5 Additional Practice

Scan for Multimedia

Leveled Practice In **1** and **2**, complete the two-way relative frequency tables.

1. Eighty students were asked, "What is your favorite color?" The two-way frequency table shows the results of the survey. Complete the two-way relative frequency table to show the distribution of the data with respect to all 80 students. Round to the nearest tenth of a percent.

Two-Way Frequency Table

		Gender		
		Boys	Girls	Total
Favorite Color	Red	18	22	40
	Blue	10	14	24
	Green	10	6	16
	Total	38	42	80

Total Two-Way Relative Frequency Table

		Gender		
		Boys	Girls	Total
Favorite Color	Red	▢ %	▢ %	▢ %
	Blue	▢ %	▢ %	▢ %
	Green	▢ %	▢ %	▢ %
	Total	▢ %	▢ %	100%

2. In a recent survey, 40 people were asked, "Do you like thunderstorms?" The two-way frequency table shows the results of the survey. Complete the row two-way relative frequency table to show the distribution of the data with respect to gender. Round to the nearest tenth of a percent.

Two-Way Frequency Table

		Like Thunderstorms?		
		Yes	No	Total
Gender	Men	12	10	22
	Women	10	8	18
	Total	22	18	40

Row Two-Way Relative Frequency Table

		Like Thunderstorms?		
		Yes	No	Total
Gender	Men	▢ %	▢ %	100%
	Women	▢ %	▢ %	100%
	Total	▢ %	▢ %	100%

3. Five hundred people in each of two cities were asked if they frequently use umbrellas. The row two-way relative frequency table shows the relative frequencies with respect to the people in each city. In which city do people use umbrellas less often? Explain.

Row Two-Way Relative Frequency Table

		Frequently Use an Umbrella?		
		Yes	No	Total
City	A	9%	91%	100%
	B	85%	15%	100%
	Total	47%	53%	100%

4. A researcher asked 85 students, "Do you prefer math or history?" The row two-way relative frequency table shows the relative frequencies with respect to the subject. Which subject is the students' favorite?

Row Two-Way Frequency Table

		Gender		
		Boys	Girls	Total
Subject	Math	57.9%	42.1%	100%
	History	42.6%	58.0%	100%
	Total	49.4%	50.6%	100%

5. **Higher Order Thinking** The same number of shoppers in two different stores at a mall were asked a survey question. The column two-way relative frequency table shows the relative frequencies with respect to the response.

   a. Compare the percentages for those who responded "Yes."

Column Two-Way Relative Frequency Table

		Response		
		Yes	No	Total
Store	1	74%	34%	50%
	2	26%	66%	50%
	Total	100%	100%	100%

   b. Is there evidence of an association between the response and the store at which shoppers were surveyed? Explain.

☑ Assessment Practice

6. The column two-way relative frequency table shows the relative frequencies of students with respect to their responses about riding a bus to school. Which of the following statements are true?

Column Two-Way Frequency Table

		Ride a Bus?		
		Yes	No	Total
Students	Grade 7	47%	46%	46.5%
	Grade 8	53%	54%	53.5%
	Total	100%	100%	100%

   ☐ 46% of seventh graders ride a bus.

   ☐ 46% of seventh graders do NOT ride a bus.

   ☐ 46% of the students who do NOT ride a bus are seventh graders.

   ☐ 53% of eighth graders ride a bus.

   ☐ 53% of eighth graders do NOT ride a bus.

   ☐ 53% of the students who ride a bus are eighth graders.

5-1 Additional Practice

1. Leveled Practice What conclusion can you make about the system of equations?

$$6y = 12x + 36$$
$$15y = 45x + 60$$

The slope of the first equation is [ ] the slope of the second equation.

The y-intercept of the first equation is [ ] the y-intercept of the second equation.

The system of equations has [ ] solution(s).

---

2. How many solutions does this system have?

$$y = 3x + 14$$
$$4y = 12x + 64$$

3. How many solutions does this system have?

$$x + 3y = 0$$
$$9y = -3x$$

---

4. Ben says this system of equations has one solution. Is he correct? Explain.

$$y = \tfrac{1}{4}x - 4$$
$$y = \tfrac{1}{4}x - 14$$

---

5. How many solutions does this system have?

$$-6x + 18y = 264$$
$$-12x - 36y = 130$$

6. How many solutions does this system have?

$$y = 4x + 5$$
$$y = -4x + 5$$

7. **Reasoning** The system of equations below shows the distance in miles, y, two trains travel in time, x. What conclusion can you make about the system of equations? Interpret your result in the context of the problem.

$$\text{Train A: } y = 1.6x + 4$$

$$\text{Train B: } 7y = 11.2x + 28$$

8. **Look for Relationships** Does this system have one solution, no solutions, or infinitely many solutions? Write another system of equations with the same number of solutions that uses the first equation only.

$$15x + 65y = 185$$

$$-12x - 52y = -148$$

9. **Higher Order Thinking** Under what circumstances does the system of equations $Ax + y = B$ and $y = Lx + M$ have no solution?

✅ Assessment Practice

10. By inspecting the equations, what can you determine about the solution(s) of this system?

$$x + 4 = y$$
$$x + 4y = 1$$

11. Choose the statement that correctly describes the number of solutions there are for this system of equations.

$$y = 3x + 2$$
$$y = 3x + 5$$

Ⓐ Infinitely many solutions, because the slopes are equal and the y-intercepts are equal.

Ⓑ Exactly one solution, because the slopes are equal but the y-intercepts are not equal.

Ⓒ No solution, because the slopes are equal but the y-intercepts are not equal.

Ⓓ Exactly one solution, because the slopes are not equal but the y-intercepts are equal.

5-2 Additional Practice

In 1 and 2, graph each system of equations to determine the solution.

1. $y = \frac{1}{2}x + 3$

   $2y = x + 6$

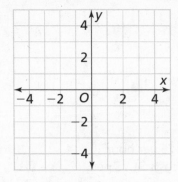

2. $y = \frac{2}{3}x + 1$

   $y = \frac{4}{3}x - 1$

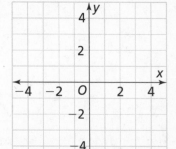

3. The cost of endless chicken wings and sauce at Restaurant X is $10. The cost of chicken wings at Restaurant Z is $0.50 per wing plus a one-time $1.50 charge for sauce. The total cost, c, of n chicken wings can be represented by a system of equations.

   a. Write the system of equations that could be used to find out the cost of n chicken wings at each restaurant.

   b. Graph the system of equations.

   c. When will the total cost of the same number of chicken wings be the same at both restaurants? Explain.

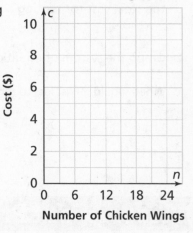

Chicken Wing Prices

4. Graph the system of equations and determine the solution.

   $6x - 3y = 3$

   $4x - 2y = 8$

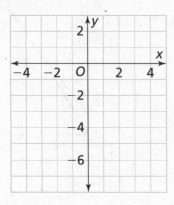

5. Graph the system of equations, and then estimate the solution.

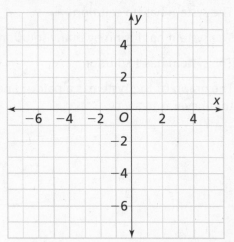

   $y = 2x + 4$

   $y = -x - 3.5$

In 6 and 7, graph and determine the solution of the system of equations.

6. $y = 6x - 3$
$\frac{1}{3}y = 2x - 1$

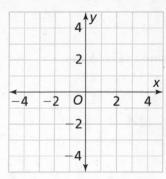

7. $y = -\frac{3}{4}x + 2$
$4y = -3x + 12$

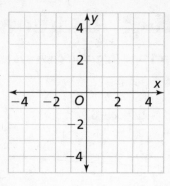

8. **Higher Order Thinking** At Bike Shop X it costs $2.75 per hour plus a $3.00 deposit to rent a bike. At Bike Shop Z it costs $1.75 per hour plus a $7.00 deposit to rent a bike.

   a. Write the system of equations that could be used to find c, the total cost for renting a bike for n hours at each shop.

   b. Graph the system of equations.

   c. When would it cost less to rent a bike from Bike Shop X? Explain.

Bike Rental Prices

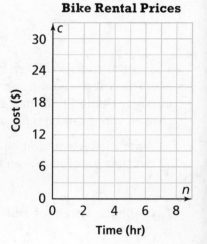

✓ Assessment Practice

9. Tickets to a play cost $12.75 per ticket plus a $12.00 fee per order online. At the box office, the cost is $15.75 per ticket. Which statement is true about the system?

   Ⓐ The system has no solution.

   Ⓑ The system has infinitely many solutions.

   Ⓒ The system has 1 solution.

   Ⓓ The graph of the system is a pair of lines that never intersect.

10. The graph of a system is shown. What is the approximate solution of the system?

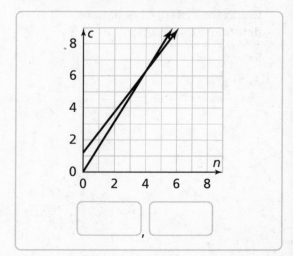

⬚ , ⬚

Name: _____

5-3 Additional Practice

1. Leveled Practice A piggy bank contains 70 coins. The coins are dimes and nickels worth $5.50. Use substitution to solve the system of equations to find how many dimes and nickels are in the piggy bank.

$$d + n = 70$$
$$0.1d + 0.05n = 5.5$$

STEP 1 Substitute for *d* to solve for *n*.

$$0.10d + 0.05n = 5.5$$

$$0.1 \cdot \left(\boxed{} \right) + 0.05n = 5.5$$

$$\boxed{} - \boxed{} + 0.05n = 5.5$$

$$7 + \boxed{} = 5.5$$

$$-0.05n = \boxed{}$$

$$n = \boxed{}$$

STEP 2 Substitute for *n* to solve for *d*.

$$d + n = 70$$

$$d + \boxed{} = 70$$

$$d = \boxed{}$$

There are $\boxed{}$ dimes and $\boxed{}$ nickels in the piggy bank.

---

2. Use substitution to solve the system of equations.

$$y = \tfrac{2}{3}x + 6$$
$$3y - 2x = 0$$

3. Use substitution to solve the system of equations.

$$y + 1 = -2x$$
$$4y + 8x = -4$$

---

4. Jake buys a fruit smoothie and a protein bar for $5.90. Kobe buys 2 fruit smoothies and 4 protein bars. He pays $16.80. What is the cost of each fruit smoothie and each protein bar?

$$x + y = 5.90$$
$$2x + 4y = 16.80$$

5. Farmer Brown planted corn and wheat on 370 acres of his land. The cost of planting and harvesting corn, *c*, is $280 per acre. The cost of planting and harvesting wheat, *w*, is $135 per acre. If Farmer Brown's total cost was $83,300, how many more acres of corn than wheat did he plant?

$$c + w = 370$$
$$280c + 135w = 83,300$$

6. a. Use substitution to solve the system of equations.

$$y = 5x + 2$$
$$12.5x + 2.5y = 5$$

b. **Reasoning** Which expression would be easier to substitute into the other equation in order to solve the problem? Explain.

7. A seed company planted a floral mosaic of a national flag. The perimeter of the rectangular planting area is 420 feet. The length of the area is 110 feet longer than the width.

a. Write a system of equations to relate the length and width of the planting area.

b. Use the system of equations to determine the length and width of the planting area.

8. **Higher Order Thinking** The system of equations relates the distance, y, from a station of two trains and the speed, x, at which they are moving.

$$y + 10x = 250$$
$$2.5y = -25x + 625$$

a. What does the system of equations tell you about the speed of the trains?

b. What does the solution tell about the locations of the trains if they left the station at the same time? If they left at different times?

✓ Assessment Practice

9. What statements are NOT true about the solution of the system?

$$y = 4x + 20$$
$$8x - 2y = -20$$

☐ The system has infinitely many solutions.

☐ $x = 5$, $y = 0$ is a solution.

☐ $x = 0$, $y = 20$ is a solution.

☐ There is no solution.

☐ There is more than one solution.

10. At a fundraiser, students sold chocolate bars with almonds and chocolate bars with walnuts. The number of chocolate bars with almonds that were sold one weekend was 3 less than 2 times the number of chocolate bars with walnuts that were sold. The number of chocolate bars with walnuts plus 4 times the number of chocolate bars with almonds was 300. How many of each kind of chocolate bar were sold that weekend?

5-4 Additional Practice

Scan for Multimedia

1. Leveled Practice Solve the system of equations using elimination.

$2x - 7y = -13$

$8x - 7y = 11$

Multiply the second equation by [ ].

$2x - 7y = -13$
$-8x + 7y = -11$
_____

[ ] + [ ] = [ ]

$x = $ [ ]

The solution is $x = $ [ ] and $y = $ [ ].

$8x - 7y = 11$

$8 \cdot ($ [ ] $) - 7y = 11$

[ ] $- 7y = 11$

$-7y = $ [ ]

$y = $ [ ]

2. Solve the system of equations using elimination.

$7x + 2y = -13$

$-7x + y = 25$

3. Solve the system of equations using elimination.

$2x + 5y = -23$

$5x + 13y = -60$

4. Two balloons, Balloon A and Balloon B, have a total volume of $\frac{3}{5}$ gallon. Balloon A has a greater volume than Balloon B. The difference of their volumes is $\frac{1}{5}$ gallon. Write and solve a system of equations using elimination to find the volume of each balloon.

5. Reasoning Suni needs to solve the system of equations using elimination.

$-5x + 3y = 15$

$2x - 3y = -15$

a. What variable should Suni solve for first? Explain.

b. Find the solution.

6. Talia is buying beads to make bracelets. She makes a bracelet with 7 plastic beads and 5 metal beads for $7.25. She makes another bracelet with 9 plastic beads and 3 metal beads for $6.75. Write and solve a system of equations using elimination to find the price of each bead.

7. Yesterday, a movie theater sold 279 bags of popcorn. A large bag of popcorn costs $4. A small bag of popcorn costs $1. In all, the movie theater made $567 from popcorn sales. Write and solve a system of equations to find how many bags of each size of popcorn were sold.

8. Brent wants to solve this system of equations using subtraction.

$$4x - 5y = 11$$

$$8x - 5y = 27$$

List the steps he should follow to solve the equations. What is the solution?

9. **Higher Order Thinking** Determine the number of solutions for this system of equations by inspection only. Explain.

$$3x - 4y = 6$$

$$12x - 16y = 24$$

☑ Assessment Practice

10. Two school groups went shopping for camping supplies at the same store. The first group spent $299 on 7 flashlights and 11 sleeping bags. The second group spent $304 on 8 flashlights and 11 sleeping bags. Write and solve a system of equations using elimination to find the price of each flashlight and each sleeping bag.

11. Solve the system of equations.

$$3y - 9x = -6$$

$$4y - 12x = -8$$

Name: _____

1. Graph $D'E'F'$, the image of triangle DEF after a translation 1 unit right and 3 units down.

2. The coordinates of $\triangle DEF$ are $D(4, 3)$, $E(7, 3)$, and $F(6, 8)$. If you translate $\triangle DEF$ 4 units left and 3 units up, what are the coordinates of F?

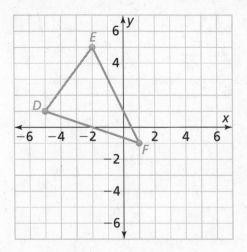

3. Quadrilateral $Q'R'S'T'$ is the image of quadrilateral $QRST$ after a translation.

   a. If the perimeter of $QRST$ is about 12.4 units, what is the perimeter of $Q'R'S'T'$?

   b. If $m\angle S = 115°$, what is $m\angle S'$?

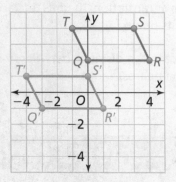

4. Quadrilateral $W'X'Y'Z'$ is a translation of quadrilateral $WXYZ$. Describe the translation.

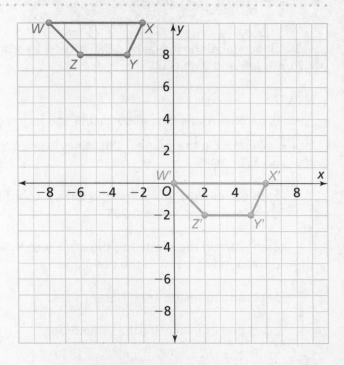

5. Is △J'K'L' a translation of △JKL Explain.

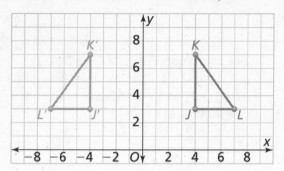

6. Quadrilateral G'R'A'M' is a translation of quadrilateral GRAM. Describe the translation.

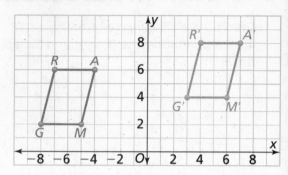

7. Higher Order Thinking The vertices of pentagon VWXYZ are V(4, 5), W(6, 5), X(6, 7), Y(5, 8), and Z(4, 7).

a. Draw VWXYZ and V'W'X'Y'Z', its image after a translation 10 units left and 2 units down.

b. Estimate the distance between V and V' to the nearest tenth.

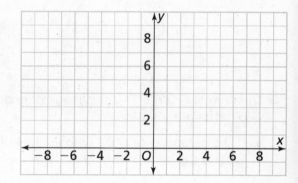

Assessment Practice

8. The vertices of △QRS are Q(3, 3), R(7, 3), and S(5, 8).

PART A

Graph and label the image of △QRS after a translation 2 units left and 2 units up.

PART B

What statements are true about △QRS and its image?

☐ Each point in the image is the same distance from each point in △QRS.

☐ Each point in the image has the same x-coordinate as the corresponding point in △QRS.

☐ Each point in the image has the same y-coordinate as the corresponding point in the preimage.

☐ △QRS and its image are different sizes.

☐ △QRS and its image are the same shape.

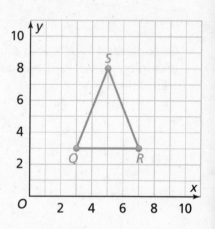

6-2 Additional Practice

Scan for Multimedia

1. Leveled Practice Rectangle *ABCD* is shown. Draw the reflection of rectangle *ABCD* across the *y*-axis.

Identify the points of the pre-image.

Identify the points of the image.

A [ ]   A' [ ]

B [ ]   B' [ ]

C [ ]   C' [ ]

D [ ]   D' [ ]

Plot the points and draw rectangle *A'B'C'D'*.

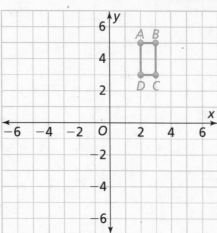

2. Reasoning Is △*E'F'G'* a reflection of △*EFG* across the line? Explain.

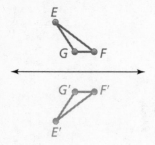

3. Consider the graph of △*ABC* and its image △*A'B'C'*. What reflection produces this image?

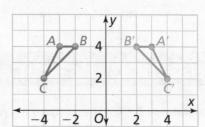

4. △*A'B'C'* is an image of △*ABC*.

a. How do the *x*-coordinates of the vertices change?

b. How do the *y*-coordinates of the vertices change?

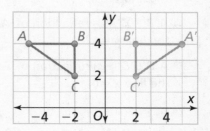

c. What reflection produces the image?

5. The vertices of △ABC are A(−5, 4), B(−2, 4), and C(−4, 2). If △ABC is reflected across the y-axis, find the coordinates of the vertex C′.

6. △E′F′G′ is the image of △EFG. What reflection produces this image?

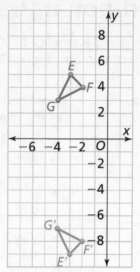

7. **Higher Order Thinking** The vertices of △ABC are A(−5, 5), B(−2, 4), and C(−4, 2). △ABC is reflected across the y-axis and then reflected again across the x-axis to produce the image △A′B′C′. What are the coordinates of △A′B′C′?

 Assessment Practice

8. Quadrilateral △A′B′C′D′ is an image of quadrilateral ABCD.

PART A

What reflection produces this image?

Ⓐ A′B′C′D′ is a reflection of ABCD across the line x = 1.

Ⓑ A′B′C′D′ is a reflection of ABCD across the line y = 0.

Ⓒ A′B′C′D′ is a reflection of ABCD across the line y = 1.

Ⓓ A′B′C′D′ is a reflection of ABCD across the line x = 0.

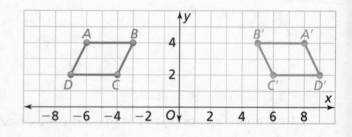

PART B

If m∠A = 110°, what is m∠A′?

Name: _____

6-3 Additional Practice

Scan for
Multimedia

1. Leveled Practice What is the angle of rotation about the origin that maps △PQR to △P'Q'R'?

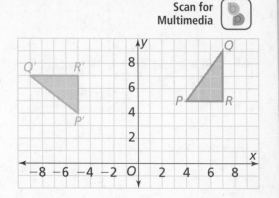

2. Is △X'Y'Z' a rotation of △XYZ? Explain.

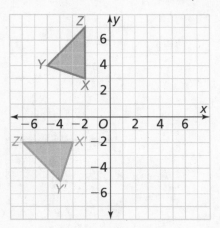

3. What is the angle of rotation about the origin that maps quadrilateral PQRS to quadrilateral P'Q'R'S'?

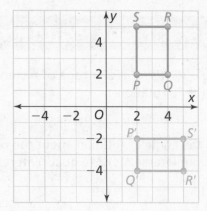

4. Pentagon JKLMN is rotated 180° about the origin. Graph and label the coordinates of pentagon J'K'L'M'N'.

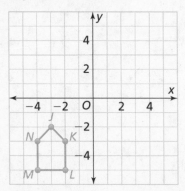

5. Is △P'Q'R' a 90° rotation of △PQR about the origin? Explain.

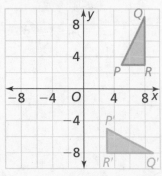

6-3 Analyze Rotations **73**

6. △*TRI* is rotated 270° about the origin. Graph and label the coordinates of △*T'R'I'*.

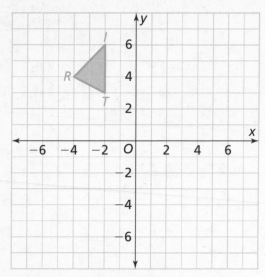

7. **Higher Order Thinking** Point *N* has coordinates (3, 4). On a quiz yesterday, Ari incorrectly claimed that if you rotate *N* 180° about the origin, the coordinates of *N'* are (−4, 3). What are the correct coordinates for *N'*? What was Ari's likely error?

☑ Assessment Practice

8. Rectangle *W'X'Y'Z'* is an image of rectangle *WXYZ* after a rotation.

PART A

What is the angle of rotation about the origin that maps quadrilateral *WXYZ* to quadrilateral *W'X'Y'Z'*?

Ⓐ 90°

Ⓑ 180°

Ⓒ 270°

Ⓓ 360°

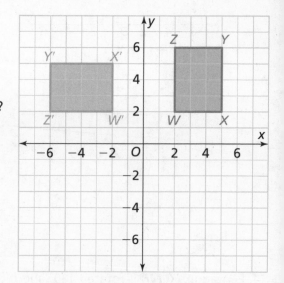

PART B

What changed when mapping quadrilateral *WXYZ* to quadrilateral *W'X'Y'Z'*?

Ⓐ size

Ⓑ shape

Ⓒ position

Ⓓ orientation

Name: _____

6-4 Additional Practice

1. Leveled Practice Describe a sequence of transformations that maps △EFG to △MNO.

A translation ☐ units left and ☐

units down, followed by a ☐

across the ☐

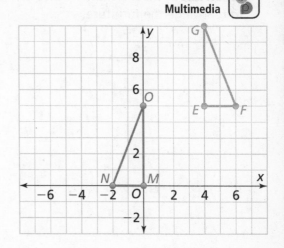

2. △D'E'F' is an image of △DEF after a sequence of transformations.

   a. Describe a sequence of transformations that maps △DEF to △D'E'F'.

   b. Describe another way that you could map △DEF to △D'E'F'.

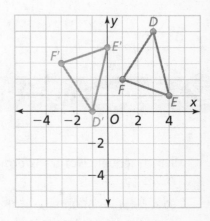

3. Map quadrilateral ABCD to quadrilateral A'B'C'D' with a rotation of 180° about the origin followed by a translation 3 units left and 7 units up.

4. Describe a sequence of transformations that maps △XYZ to △X'Y'Z'.

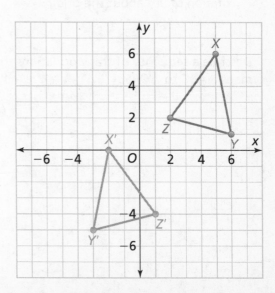

5. Higher Order Thinking A small store is rearranging their furniture. Describe the sequences of transformations they can use to rearrange the furniture.

6. Map quadrilateral *ABCD* to quadrilateral *HIJK* with a reflection across the *x*-axis followed by a translation 4 units left and 2 units down.

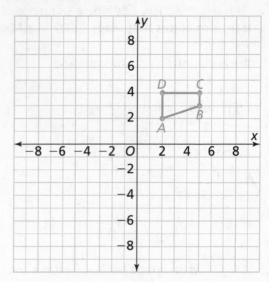

7. PART A

Which sequence of transformations maps △*QRS* to △*ABC*?

Ⓐ A rotation of 90° about the origin, followed by a translation 3 units left.

Ⓑ A reflection across the *x*-axis, followed by a rotation of 90° about the origin.

Ⓒ A rotation of 90° about the origin, followed by a reflection across the *y*-axis.

Ⓓ A reflection across the *x*-axis, followed by a rotation of 90° about the origin.

PART B

Describe a sequence of transformations that maps △*ABC* to △*QRS*.

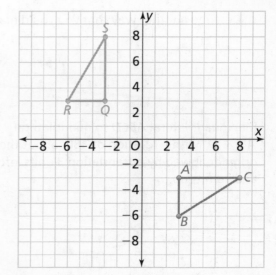

6-5 Additional Practice

1. Leveled Practice △D′E′F′ is the image of △DEF after a
reflection across the x-axis and a translation 6 units left
and 6 units up. Is the image the same size and shape as
the pre-image? Explain.

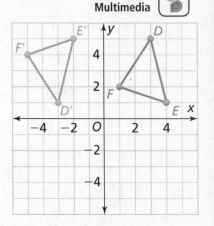

A reflection [   ] change the size and shape of
the figure.

A translation [   ] change the size and shape of
the figure.

△DEF and △D′E′F′ [   ] the same size and shape.

2. Which two triangles are congruent? Describe a
sequence of transformations that maps one
figure onto the other.

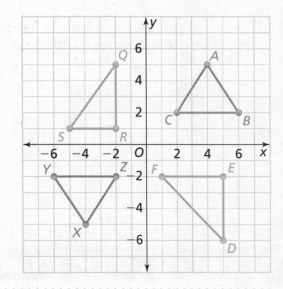

3. Is ABCD ≅ A′B′C′D′? Explain.

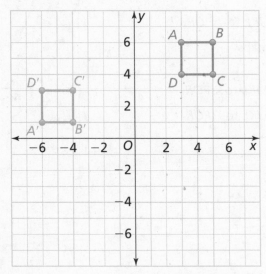

4. Construct Arguments Describe a way to
show △DEF is congruent to △D′E′F′.

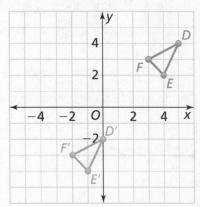

5. How can you decide if △DEF ≅ △D'E'F'?

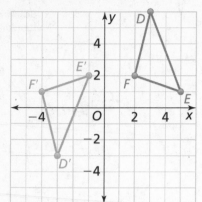

6. Is ABCDE ≅ VWXYZ? Explain.

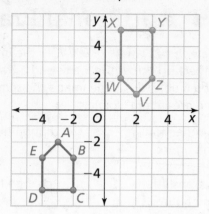

7. Higher Order Thinking Describe a sequence of transformations that maps quadrilateral ABCD onto A'B'C'D'.

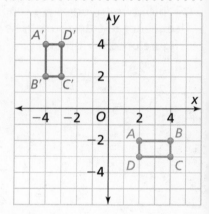

Assessment Practice

8. PART A

How can you determine whether △JKL ≅ △PQR?

Ⓐ Decide whether a sequence of rotations maps △JKL to △PQR.

Ⓑ Decide whether a sequence of transformations maps △JKL to △PQR.

Ⓒ Decide whether a sequence of translations maps △JKL to △PQR.

Ⓓ Decide whether a sequence of reflections maps △JKL to △PQR.

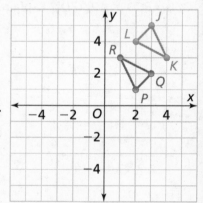

PART B

Is △JKL ≅ △PQR? Explain.

6-6 Additional Practice

1. Leveled Practice Draw the image of △ABC after a dilation with center (0, 0) and scale factor $\frac{1}{4}$.

Find the coordinates of each point in the original figure.

A: (⬜), (⬜)

B: (⬜), (⬜)

C: (⬜), (⬜)

Multiply each coordinate by ⬜ .

Find the coordinates of each point in the image:

A′: (⬜), (⬜)

B′: (⬜), (⬜)

C′: (⬜), (⬜)

Graph the image.

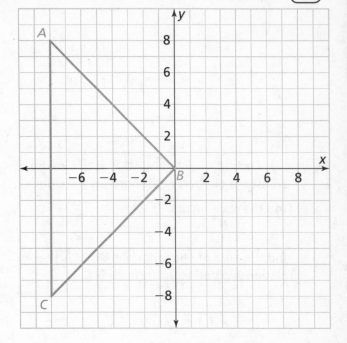

2. △RST has vertices R(0, 0), S(6, 3), and T(3, −3). △R′S′T′ is the image of △RST after a dilation with center (0, 0) and scale factor $\frac{1}{3}$. What are the coordinates of point S′?

3. Rectangle QUAD has coordinates Q(4, 5), U(4, 10), A(11, 10), and D(11, 5). Q′U′A′D′ is the image of QUAD after a dilation with center (0, 0) and scale factor 5. What is the length of segment Q′U′?

4. The graph shows △KJL and △K′J′L′, its image after a dilation.

   a. Is this dilation an enlargement or a reduction? Explain.

   b. Find the scale factor of the dilation.

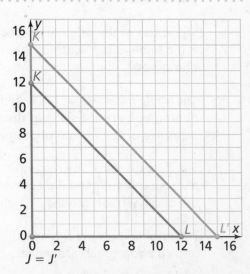

5. Draw the image of △PQR after a dilation with center (0, 0) and scale factor 3.

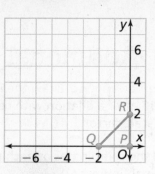

6. **Higher Order Thinking** △P'Q'R' is the image of △PQR after a dilation with center at the origin.

   a. Find the scale factor.

   b. Find the area of each triangle. What is the relationship between the areas?

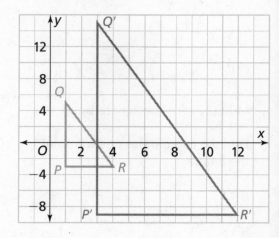

☑ Assessment Practice

7. A photographer uses a computer program to resize a photograph by a scale factor of $\frac{2}{3}$. What is true about the resized photograph? Select all that apply.

   ☐ The length of the original photograph is the same as the length of the resized photograph.

   ☐ The width of the original photograph is the same as the width of the resized photograph.

   ☐ The angle measures of the original photograph are the same as the angle measures of the resized photograph.

   ☐ The dimensions of the resized photograph are $\frac{2}{3}$ the dimensions of the original photograph.

   ☐ The original photograph and the resized photograph are similar.

8. Is the dilation an enlargement or a reduction? Explain.

6-7 Additional Practice

1. Leveled Practice *ABCD* and *EFGH* are quadrilaterals. Given *ABCD* ~ *EFGH*, describe a sequence of transformations that maps *ABCD* to *EFGH*

• Reflection across the ☐

• Translation ☐ unit(s) right

 and ☐ unit(s) up

• Dilation with center (0, 0) and scale

 factor ☐

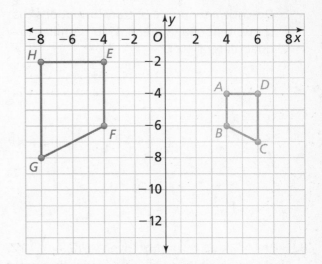

2. a. If △*PQR* were similar to △*XYZ*, what angle would correspond to ∠*Q*?

b. Are the triangles similar? Explain.

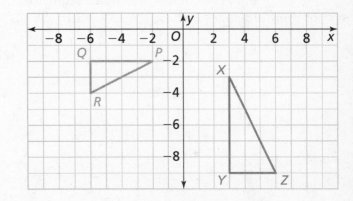

3. Quadrilateral *RSTU* is translated 6 units right and 4 units up, and then dilated with center of dilation (0, 0) and scale factor $\frac{1}{2}$. Graph the resulting similar quadrilateral *VXYZ*.

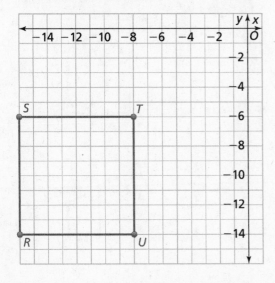

4. Describe a sequence of transformations that shows that △*NOP* is similar to △*QRS*.

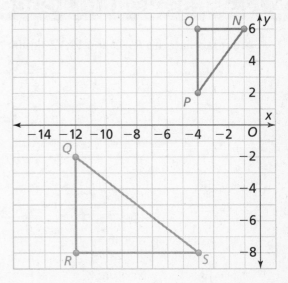

5. Quadrilateral *RSTU* ~ quadrilateral *VXYZ*.

   a. Which angle corresponds to ∠S?

   b. Describe a sequence of transformations that shows that quadrilateral *RSTU* is similar to quadrilateral *VXYZ*.

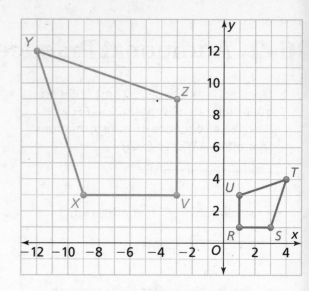

6. **Higher Order Thinking** Given △*JKL* ~ △*XYZ*. Find two possible coordinates for missing point *Y*. For each coordinate chosen, describe a sequence of transformations that could map △*JKL* to △*XYZ*.

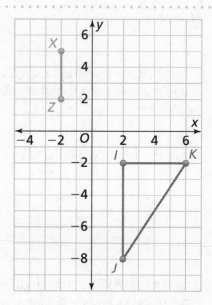

☑ Assessment Practice

7. Are quadrilaterals *RSTU* and *VXYZ* similar? Explain.

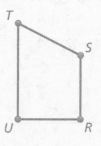

6-8 Additional Practice

Scan for Multimedia

1. Leveled Practice If $p\|q$, what is the value of v?

∠u and ∠v are [   ] angles.

So, ∠u and ∠v are [   ].

m∠v is [   ].

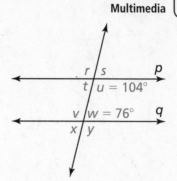

2. Are ∠6 and ∠7 corresponding angles if $a\|b$ and $c\|d$? Explain.

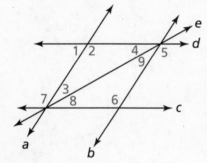

3. Find $m\angle v$ given that $p\|q$, $m\angle u = 75.8°$, and $m\angle w = 104.2°$.

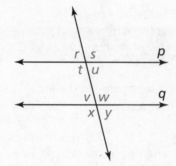

4. In the figure $m\|n$. What is the value of x?

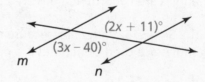

$(2x + 11)°$

$(3x - 40)°$

5. Reasoning What value of x will show that line m is parallel to line n? Explain.

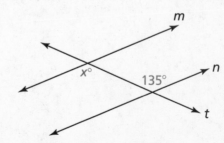

$x°$

$135°$

6. **Higher Order Thinking** Determine which lines, if any, in the figure are parallel.

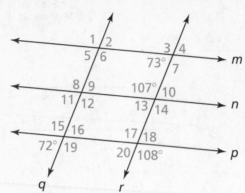

7. In the figure $d \parallel m$. What is the value of x?

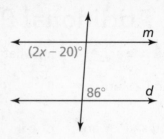

☑ Assessment Practice

8. Which congruence statements show that $m \parallel n$? Select all that apply.

☐ If $\angle 9 \cong \angle 13$, then $m \parallel n$ because if corresponding angles are congruent, lines are parallel.

☐ If $\angle 4 \cong \angle 5$, then $m \parallel n$ because if alternate interior angles are congruent, lines are parallel.

☐ If $\angle 12 \cong \angle 13$, then $m \parallel n$ because if alternate interior angles are congruent, lines are parallel.

☐ If $\angle 5 \cong \angle 15$, then $m \parallel n$ because if corresponding angles are congruent, lines are parallel.

☐ If $\angle 10 \cong \angle 14$, then $m \parallel n$ because if alternate interior angles are congruent, lines are parallel.

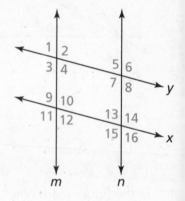

9. In the figure, $a \parallel b$. Given $m\angle x = 147.2°$ and $m\angle y = 32.8°$, find the measures of $\angle u$ and $\angle q$. Explain your reasoning.

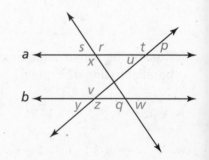

6-9 Additional Practice

Scan for
Multimedia

1. Leveled Practice For the figure shown, find $m\angle 1$.

∠1 is a [   ] of the 119° angle.

The 119° angle is equal to the sum of its [   ].

So, $m\angle 1 = $ [   ] – [   ].

$m\angle 1 = $ [   ]

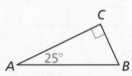

119°   57°

---

2. Find $m\angle B$ for the triangle shown.

C

25°   B
A

3. Find $m\angle R$.

S

$(x + 70)°$

$x°$ $(x + 20)°$
Q   R

---

4. Reasoning Can you find the $m\angle 1$ without using remote interior angles? Explain.

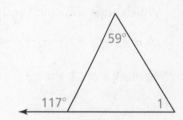

59°

117°   1

---

5. Find the value of x in the triangle.

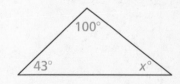

100°

43° $x°$

6. **Higher Order Thinking** Given that $m\angle A = (16x)°$, $m\angle C = (8x + 20)°$, and $m\angle D = 128°$, what is $m\angle B$?

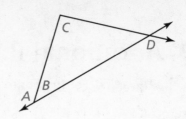

✓ Assessment Practice

7. The measure of $\angle 6$ is 120°. The measure of $\angle 5$ is 100°. What is the measure of $\angle 4$?

   Ⓐ 140

   Ⓑ 80

   Ⓒ 60

   Ⓓ 40

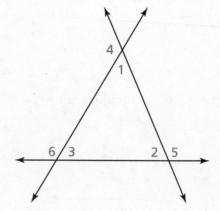

8. In the figure, $m\angle 1 = (5x + 11)°$, $m\angle 2 = (3x + 22)°$, and $m\angle 3 = (9x + 28)°$.

   PART A

   Which equation could you use to find $m\angle 1$?

   Ⓐ $m\angle 1 + m\angle 2 + m\angle 3 = 90°$

   Ⓑ $m\angle 1 + m\angle 2 + m\angle 3 = 180°$

   Ⓒ $m\angle 1 - m\angle 2 = m\angle 3$

   Ⓓ $m\angle 1 + m\angle 2 = m\angle 3$

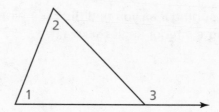

   PART B

   What is $m\angle 1$, in degrees?

6-10 Additional Practice

Scan for Multimedia

1. Leveled Practice Is △XYZ ~ △XJK?

Find m∠K.

m∠K = [ ]

m∠K = [ ]

m∠K = [ ]

△XYZ and △XJK [ ] similar because

there [ ] two congruent angles.

2. If △ABC and △EDC are similar, what is the value of x?

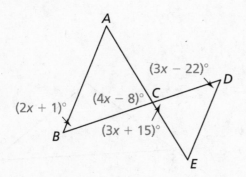

3. Is △XYZ ~ △GHI? Explain.

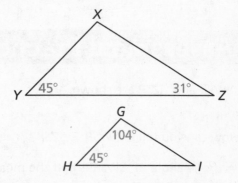

4. Construct Arguments Is △QRT ~ △GHI? Explain.

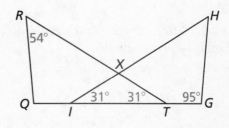

5. Is $\triangle TUV \sim \triangle WXV$? Explain.

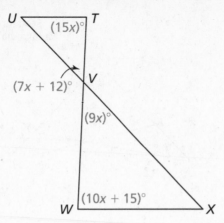

6. Higher Order Thinking Are the triangles similar? Explain.

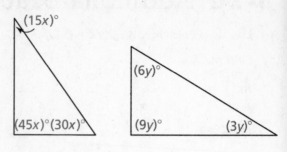

☑ Assessment Practice

7. $\triangle WSR$ and $\triangle ZSP$ are shown.

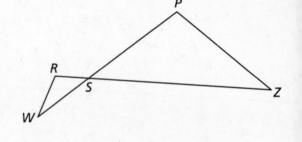

PART A

How can you tell if $\triangle WSR \sim \triangle ZSP$?

Ⓐ If one angle of $\triangle WSR$ is half the measure of one angle of $\triangle ZSP$

Ⓑ If two angles of $\triangle WSR$ are proportional to two angles of $\triangle ZSP$

Ⓒ If two angles of $\triangle WSR$ are congruent to two angles of $\triangle ZSP$

Ⓓ If one angle of $\triangle WSR$ is congruent to one angle of $\triangle ZSP$

PART B

If $\angle R = 110°$, $\angle Z = 35°$ and $\angle PST = 40°$, is $\triangle WSR \sim \triangle ZSP$? Explain your reasoning.

Name: _____

7-1 Additional Practice

Leveled Practice In **1** and **2**, find the missing side length of each triangle.

1.

15, c, 36

2.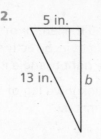

5 in., 13 in., b

$\boxed{}^2 + 36\boxed{} = c^2$

$\boxed{} + \boxed{} = c^2$

$\sqrt{\boxed{}} = \sqrt{\boxed{}}$

$c = \boxed{}$

The length of the hypotenuse is $\boxed{}$ units.

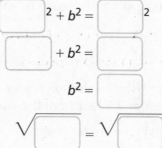

$\boxed{}^2 + b^2 = \boxed{}^2$

$\boxed{} + b^2 = \boxed{}$

$b^2 = \boxed{}$

$\sqrt{\boxed{}} = \sqrt{\boxed{}}$

$b = \boxed{}$

The length of leg b is $\boxed{}$ inches.

3. What is the length of side a rounded to the nearest tenth of a centimeter?

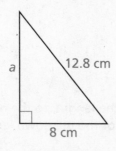

a, 12.8 cm, 8 cm

4. What is the length of side c rounded to the nearest tenth of an inch?

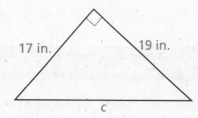

17 in., 19 in., c

5. Two dimensions of a right triangle are 5 units and 13 units. A student writes the equation $5^2 + 13^2 = c^2$ to find the length of the third side.

a. If all the side lengths are integers, is the student's equation correct? Explain.

b. If the student is incorrect, write an equation that will give the length of the third side, and show that the equation is correct.

6. What is the length of the hypotenuse of the triangle when $x = 3$? Round your answer to the nearest tenth.

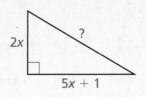

7. A student was asked to find the length of the unknown leg of the right triangle. The student incorrectly said that the length of the unknown leg of the right triangle is about 6.2 centimeters.

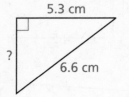

   a. Find the length of the unknown leg of the right triangle to the nearest tenth of a centimeter.

   b. What mistake might the student have made?

8. **Higher Order Thinking** Dillon places a ladder against a wall. The base of the ladder is 5 feet from the wall. The ladder is 12 feet long.

   a. How high will the ladder reach?

   b. How will shortening the distance between the base of the ladder and the wall affect the dimensions of the triangle they form? Explain in terms of the Pythagorean Theorem.

☑ Assessment Practice

9. What is the length, in inches, of the hypotenuse of the right triangle?

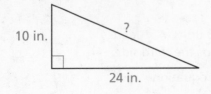

10. What is the length, to the nearest tenth of a meter, of the unknown leg of the right triangle?

Name: _____

PRACTICE   TUTORIAL

Scan for
Multimedia

Leveled Practice In **1** and **2**, determine whether each triangle is a right triangle.

1.

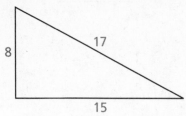

$$a^2 + b^2 = c^2$$

$$\boxed{}^2 + \boxed{}^2 \stackrel{?}{=} \boxed{}^2$$

$$\boxed{} + \boxed{} \stackrel{?}{=} \boxed{}$$

$$\boxed{} \bigcirc \boxed{}$$

Is the triangle a right triangle? $\boxed{}$

2.

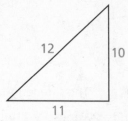

$$a^2 + b^2 = c^2$$

$$\boxed{}^2 + \boxed{}^2 \stackrel{?}{=} \boxed{}^2$$

$$\boxed{} + \boxed{} \stackrel{?}{=} \boxed{}$$

$$\boxed{} \bigcirc \boxed{}$$

Is the triangle a right triangle? $\boxed{}$

---

3. Model with Math $\triangle LMN$ is an equilateral triangle. Is $\overline{MQ}$ the height of $\triangle LMN$? Explain.

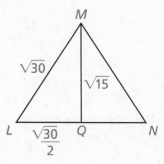

4. The side lengths of three triangles are shown. Which of the triangles are right triangles?

Triangle	Side Lengths		
1	20	$\sqrt{425}$	5
2	14	21	10
3	$\frac{6}{11}$	$\frac{8}{11}$	$\frac{10}{11}$

5. The length of one leg of a right triangle is 8 centimeters shorter than the hypotenuse. The hypotenuse is 42 centimeters. What is the length of the unknown leg of the right triangle rounded to the nearest tenth?

6. Model with Math △*ABC* is an isosceles triangle. Is $\overline{AD}$ the height of △*ABC*? Explain.

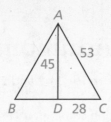

---

7. Higher Order Thinking The side lengths of three triangles are given.

Triangle 1: $\sqrt{519}$ units, 27 units, $\sqrt{210}$ units

Triangle 2: 21 units, $\sqrt{109}$ units, $\sqrt{420}$ units

Triangle 3: $\sqrt{338}$ units, 26 units, $\sqrt{338}$ units

a. Which lengths represent the side lengths of a right triangle? Explain.

b. For any triangles that are not right triangles, use any two of the sides to make a right triangle. Explain.

✓ Assessment Practice

8. Is △*ABC* a right triangle? Explain.

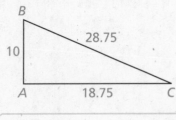

9. Which lengths represent the side lengths of a right triangle?

Triangle 1: 4, 6, 10

Triangle 2: 6, 8, 10

Triangle 3: 10, 24, 26

Ⓐ Triangle 1 and Triangle 3 are right triangles.

Ⓑ Triangle 2 and Triangle 3 are right triangles.

Ⓒ All of the triangles are right triangles.

Ⓓ None of the triangles are right triangles.

Name: _____

7-3 Additional Practice

Scan for Multimedia

Leveled Practice In **1** and **2**, use the Pythagorean Theorem to solve.

1. A shipping company uses an inclined conveyor belt to load and unload packages. The dock is 15 feet above the ground. The base of the conveyor belt is 40 feet from the dock. What is the length of the conveyor belt? Round to the nearest tenth of a foot.

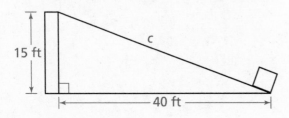

15 ft

c

40 ft

$$a^2 + b^2 = c^2$$

$$\boxed{}^2 + \boxed{}^2 = \boxed{}^2$$

$$\boxed{} + \boxed{} = \boxed{}$$

$$\boxed{} = \boxed{}$$

$$\boxed{} \approx \boxed{}$$

The length of the conveyor belt is about $\boxed{}$ feet.

2. Find the missing lengths in the rectangular prism.

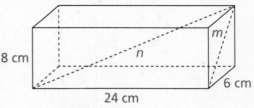

8 cm   n   m

24 cm   6 cm

$$a^2 + b^2 = c^2$$

$$\boxed{}^2 + \boxed{}^2 = \boxed{}^2$$

$$\boxed{} + \boxed{} = \boxed{}$$

$$\boxed{} = \boxed{}$$

$$\boxed{} = \boxed{}$$

$$a^2 + b^2 = c^2$$

$$\boxed{}^2 + \boxed{}^2 = \boxed{}^2$$

$$\boxed{} + \boxed{} = \boxed{}$$

$$\boxed{} = \boxed{}$$

$$\boxed{} = \boxed{}$$

3. A square table in the cafeteria has the dimensions shown. What is the length of the diagonal of the table? Round to the nearest hundredth of a foot.

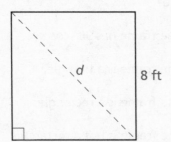

d   8 ft

4. **Reasoning** What is the measurement of the longest line segment in a right rectangular prism that is 26 inches long, 2 inches wide, and 2 inches tall? Round to the nearest tenth of an inch.

5. **Make Use of Structure** Li needs to find the height of the rectangular prism, x. He knows that $d = 15$ mm. If he also knows the measure of line a, can he find the measure of x? Explain.

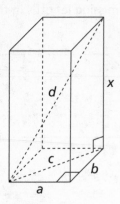

6. Sasha is building a tree house. The walls are 6.5 feet tall and she is using a brace to hold up the wall while she nails it to the floor. The brace is 8 feet long and she has positioned it 5 feet from the wall. Does her wall meet the floor at a right angle? Explain.

7. **Higher Order Thinking** An eight-sided game piece is shaped like two identical square pyramids attached at their bases. The perimeters of the square bases are 80 millimeters, and the slant height of each pyramid is 17 millimeters. What is the length of the game piece? Round to the nearest tenth of a millimeter.

✅ Assessment Practice

8. What are the dimensions, to the nearest meter, of the prism?

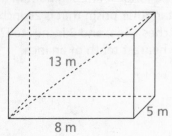

Ⓐ 5 m × 8 m × 8 m

Ⓑ 5 m × 8 m × 9 m

Ⓒ 5 m × 8 m × 10 m

Ⓓ 5 m × 8 m × 11 m

9. Carlos is making a wood picture frame. The picture frame is 11 inches by 14 inches. After nailing the frame together, Carlos measures the diagonal. If the diagonal is 19 inches long, what is true about the frame?

Ⓐ The frame has 90° corners.

Ⓑ The frame is a triangle.

Ⓒ The frame is a rectangle.

Ⓓ The frame is not a rectangle.

7-4 Additional Practice

1. Leveled Practice Use the Pythagorean Theorem to find the distance between points P and Q. Round to the nearest tenth.

Label the length, in units, of each leg of the right triangle.

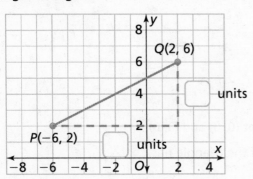

□ units

□ units

$c^2 = \boxed{}^2 + \boxed{}^2$

$c = \sqrt{\boxed{}}$

The distance between point P and point Q is about $\boxed{}$ units.

---

2. Find the perimeter of triangle XYZ. Round to the nearest hundredth.

3. Determine whether the triangle is equilateral, isosceles, or scalene.

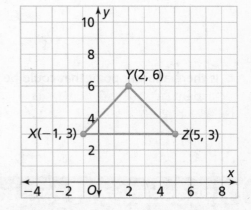

---

4. A shopper drives from the mall at point M to the post office located at point P. What distance does the shopper drive?

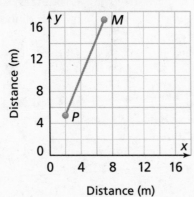

5. Is point $K(10, 16)$ or point $L(12, 12)$ closer to point $J(6, 4)$? Explain.

6. **Use Structure** Point B has coordinates (−4, −2). The x-coordinate of point A is 5. The distance between point A and point B is 15 units.

   a. What are the possible coordinates of point A?

   b. Find the possible coordinates of point A if point B were moved to (−7, −2).

7. The coordinates of triangle EFG are E(28, 24), F(24, 27), and G(0, 24).

   a. What is the perimeter of triangle EFG? Round to the nearest tenth.

   b. Is the triangle equilateral, isosceles, or scalene?

8. **Higher Order Thinking** There are points on a grid at (0, 0) and (3, 0).

   a. What is a possible coordinate of the third vertex if the triangle has a perimeter of 11 units? Explain.

   b. Is there another point that could be the third vertex? Explain.

☑ Assessment Practice

9. Find the distance, in units, between P and Q. Round to the nearest tenth.

   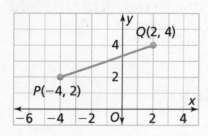

10. Find the distance, in units, between S(2.3, 4.8) and T(6.4, 7.9). Round to the nearest tenth.

Name: _____

8-1 Additional Practice

Scan for Multimedia

1. What is the surface area of the cylinder? Use 3.14 for π, and round to the nearest tenth.

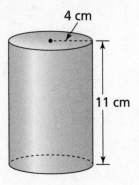

4 cm

11 cm

2. What is the surface area of the ball shown? Use $\frac{22}{7}$ for π, and round to the nearest whole number.

Radius is 9 centimeters.

3. The length of the radius and slant height of two different cones are shown.

a. Find the surface area of each cone. Use 3.14 for π, and round to the nearest hundredth.

b. Which cone has the greater surface area?

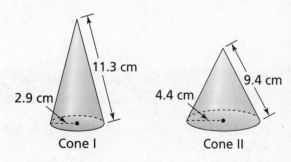

11.3 cm

2.9 cm

Cone I

9.4 cm

4.4 cm

Cone II

4. A sphere has a surface area of 9,244 square feet.

a. What is the radius of the sphere? Use 3.14 for π, and round to the nearest hundredth.

b. **Make Sense and Persevere** How can you check your answer?

5. Sergio works at a bakery and needs to cover eight identical cylindrical cakes with frosting. The bottom of each cake does not need frosting. What surface area of each cake needs to be frosted? Use 3.14 for π, and round to the nearest hundredth.

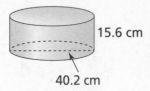

15.6 cm

40.2 cm

6. What is the surface area of the cone? Use 3.14 for π, and round to the nearest whole number.

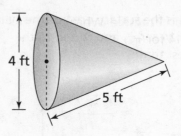

4 ft

5 ft

7. **Higher Order Thinking** A cylindrical vase has height 17 inches and radius 3 inches.

   a. Find the exact surface area of the vase in terms of π.

   b. Suppose a second vase has double the radius, but the same surface area. What is the height of the vase?

8. A welder is making a metal sphere. The radius will be 115 centimeters. What is the surface area of the metal sphere? Use 3.14 for π.

   Ⓐ About 166,106 cm²

   Ⓑ About 52,900 cm²

   Ⓒ About 664,424 cm²

   Ⓓ About 41,526.5 cm²

9. Thirty percent of the metal sphere from Exercise 8 will be covered in a metal that is tinted red. What is the area, to the nearest square centimeter, of the tinted section of the sphere?

8-2 Additional Practice

1. Leveled Practice What is the volume of the cylinder? Use 3.14 for π.

$V = \pi \cdot \boxed{}^2 \cdot \boxed{}$

$= \pi \cdot \boxed{} \cdot \boxed{}$

$= \boxed{} \pi$

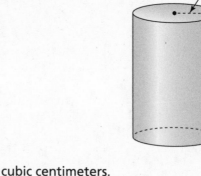

4 cm

11 cm

The volume of the cylinder is about $\boxed{}$ cubic centimeters.

---

2. The volume of the cylinder is 48π cubic feet. The area of the base is 12π square feet. What is the height of the cylinder?

3. You are building a sand castle and want to use a cylindrical bucket that holds 885 cubic inches of sand. If the bucket has a height of 11.7 inches, what is the radius of the bucket? Use 3.14 for π, and round to the nearest tenth.

---

4. A cylinder has radius 2.3 inches and height 5.5 inches.

   a. Find the volume of the cylinder. Use 3.14 for π, and round to the nearest tenth.

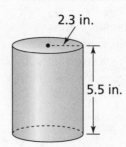

2.3 in.

5.5 in.

   b. **Reasoning** If the radius of the cylinder is changed, but the height remains the same, how will the volume change?

5. **Critique Reasoning** Claire says that she can find the volume of any cylinder as long as she can measure the circumference and height. Is Claire correct? Explain.

6. Find the volume of each cylinder in terms of π. Which cylinder has the greatest volume?

   Cylinder A: diameter = 7 in., height = 12 in.

   Cylinder B: diameter = 12 in., height = 7 in.

7. **Higher Order Thinking** The cylinder shown is a steel tube that weighs 0.2835 pound per cubic inch. The inner part of the tube is hollow. What is the weight of the tube? Use 3.14 for π, and round to the nearest tenth.

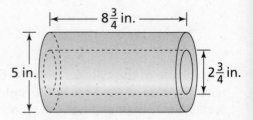

✓ Assessment Practice

8. The diameter of a cylinder is $(6x - 8)$ in. and the height of the cylinder is $(11x + 10)$ in. Find the volume, in cubic inches and in terms of π, of the cylinder when $x = 7$.

9. The volume of a cylinder is $4{,}000\pi$ in.^{3}. The height of the cylinder is 250 in. What is the radius, in inches, of the cylinder?

8-3 Additional Practice

Scan for
Multimedia

Leveled Practice In **1** and **2**, find the volume of each cone.

1. What is the volume of the cone? Use 3.14 for π.

$V \approx \frac{1}{3}(3.14)()^2()$

$V = \frac{1}{3}(3.14)()()$

$V = \frac{1}{3}()$

$V = $ units^3

45

20

2. Find the volume of the cone. Use $\frac{22}{7}$ for π.

$V \approx \frac{1}{3}\left(\frac{22}{7}\right)()^2()$

$V = \frac{1}{3}\left(\frac{22}{7}\right)()()$

$V = \frac{1}{3}\left(\frac{22}{7}\right)()$

$V = $ in.^{3}

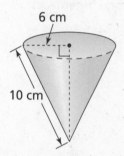

6 in.   14 in.

3. A trap to catch fruit flies uses a cone in a jar. The cone is shown.

a. What is the volume of the cone? Write your answer in terms of π.

b. **Reasoning** Explain why an answer in terms of π is more accurate than an answer that uses 3.14 for π.

6 cm

10 cm

4. An artist makes a small cone-shaped sculpture for his class. The circumference of the sculpture is 3.14 feet. What is the volume of the sculpture? Use 3.14 for π.

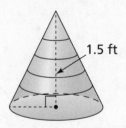

1.5 ft

5. The cone has a volume of 15,225π cubic millimeters. What is the radius of the base?

203 mm

6. The volume of a cone is 763.02 cubic inches. The radius and height of the cone are equal. What is the radius of the cone? Use 3.14 for π.

7. What is the volume of the cone? Use 3.14 for π.

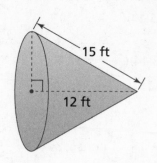

35 m

37 m

8. a. What is the volume of the cone? Use 3.14 for π.

15 ft

12 ft

   b. **Reasoning** Mario says that the volume of the cone is 1,271.7 cubic feet. What error did he likely make?

9. A cone has a height of 14 centimeters and a base with a circumference of 8.4π centimeters. What is the volume of the cone in terms of π?

10. **Higher Order Thinking** A cone has a radius of 39 centimeters and a slant height of 65 centimeters.

    a. What is the volume of the cone in terms of π?

    b. **Reasoning** If the radius is now half the size and the height is the same, how has the volume of the cone changed?

11. List the cones described below in order from least volume to greatest volume.

    • Cone 1: radius 16 cm and height 12 cm
    • Cone 2: radius 12 cm and height 16 cm
    • Cone 3: radius 8 cm and height 24 cm

    Ⓐ Cone 1, Cone 2, Cone 3

    Ⓑ Cone 2, Cone 1, Cone 3

    Ⓒ Cone 3, Cone 2, Cone 1

    Ⓓ Cone 3, Cone 1, Cone 2

12. What is the volume, in cubic inches, of a cone that has a radius of 9 inches and a height of 16 inches? Use 3.14 for π, and round to the nearest hundredth.

PRACTICE   TUTORIAL

8-4 Additional Practice

Scan for
Multimedia

1. **Leveled Practice** A solid plastic sphere has a radius of 8 inches. How much plastic does it take to make one sphere? Use 3.14 for π, and round to the nearest whole number.

Use the formula $V = \frac{4}{3}\pi r^3$.

$$V = \frac{4}{3}\pi(\boxed{}^3)$$

$$V = \frac{4}{3}\pi(\boxed{})$$

$$V \approx \frac{4}{3}(\boxed{})(\boxed{})$$

$$V \approx (\boxed{})$$

It takes approximately $\boxed{}$ cubic inches of plastic to make one sphere.

2. A sphere has a diameter of 0.926 inch.

   a. What is the volume of the sphere? Use 3.14 for π, and round to the nearest thousandth.

   b. **Reasoning** How does the volume of this sphere compare to the volume of a sphere with radius 0.926 inch?

3. Find the volume of the figure. Use 3.14 for π, and round to the nearest whole number.

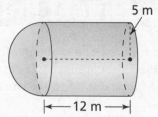

5 m

12 m

4. A spherical container has surface area of about 5,538.96 square centimeters.

   a. What is the volume of the container? Use 3.14 for π, and round to the nearest hudredth.

   b. **Make Sense and Persevere** If 600 cubic centimeters of water flow into the container in one minute, about how many minutes will it take to fill the container?

5. A sphere has a radius of 19 inches.

   a. What is the volume of the sphere? Use 3.14 for π, and round to the nearest hundredth.

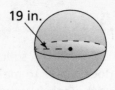

   b. Describe how the volume of the sphere changes if the radius is increased by 1.

6. **Higher Order Thinking** Find the volume of the solid where the two hemispheres are hollow. Explain. Use 3.14 for π, and round to the nearest hundredth.

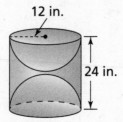

12 in.

24 in.

![Assessment Practice]

✅ Assessment Practice

7. The surface area of a globe in Mr. Patton's classroom is about 452.39 square inches. Find its volume in cubic inches. Use 3.14 for π. Round to the nearest whole number.

8. A septic tank has the shape shown. How many gallons of fluid does it hold? Use 3.14 for π, and round to the nearest gallon. Note: 1 ft^3 ≈ 7.48 gal.

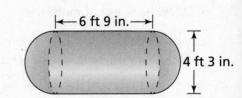

|←— 6 ft 9 in. —→|

4 ft 3 in.